MIRACLES BEYOND THE CROWD

MIRACLES BEYOND
THE CROWD

NICO SMIT

Copyright © 2025 by Nico Smit

Nico Smit's blog: nicosmitblog.com

All rights reserved. No part of this book may be reproduced in any manner whatsoever without written permission except in the case of brief quotations embodied in critical articles and reviews.
First Printing by Ingram Spark, 2025

A copy of this title, Miracles Beyond the Crowd, is held at the National Library of Australia.

ISBN: 978-1-7641247-5-1
eISBN: 978-1-7641247-6-8

Scripture taken from the New King James Version®. Copyright © 1982 by Thomas Nelson. Used by permission. All rights reserved.

Published by Bekker Media on behalf of Yeshua Collective, Pty Ltd,
58 Channel Highway, Kingston TAS 7050.

Cover design by Matthew de Livera, @mdfilmcreative
Edited by Bekker Media, New South Wales, Australia
www.bekkermedia.com

Contents

Endorsements — vii
Foreword — xiii

PROLOGUE — 1

Introduction — 3

1 Faith And The Making Of Miracles — 9
2 Rip Open The Roof! — 21
3 When The Table Feeds The Uninvited — 31
4 Open The Door For Jesus — 45
5 When Worship Breaks The Room — 57
6 Don't Die Before Your Time — 73
7 Loss At The Gate — 81
8 Sticking With Jesus — 95

Conclusion — 109

Other Books by Nico Smit — 115

Endorsements

Nico, you don't write books to read, instead every page reads you. Every line of this book is a challenge and conviction that requires an answer. Nothing is left the same. Every page is an explosive encounter to go beyond where you are. Jesus loved the crowds, He had compassion on the crowds, but He met the needs of those who refused to remain in the crowds, those who were desperate enough to move beyond for the more of God.

Not all crowds are equal! There are crowds that paralyze, some criticize, some demoralize while others neutralize. Crowds can be fickle moving from adoration to condemnation in a moment as we see in the life of Jesus. We live among these crowds.

This book brings Jesus from the pages of the Bible to your front door. Just like Jesus came to Zachaeus and said "I MUST" come to your house. Jesus is waiting to move you from beyond the religious-routine--rut experiences to renewal, refreshing and restoration.

The miracles of God are waiting for you beyond the crowd. This is another comfort-zone wrecking book by Nico. It should come with highlighters and pencils included! It is impossible to simply read it with your eyes. I am honored to recommend it.

Shane Cooke, Melbourne, Australia
International Preacher, Equipper and pastor
Shane Cooke Ministries

I couldn't put it down! In *Miracles Beyond the Crowd*, Nico Smit unveils a Jesus who still heals today! With wisdom, revelation, and deep pastoral insight, he invites us to step out of complacency and into courageous faith.

Nico writes, "That's often the dividing line. Some wait for healing to find them, others pursue it. And the ones who pursue it usually do so not because they're stronger, but because they've come to the end of everything else."

It's in that sacred place—at the end of ourselves—that a new journey begins: one of freedom, restoration, and yes, miracles. This book will challenge, inspire, and equip you to believe again and receive everything Jesus purchased for you on the cross. Enjoy!

Elijah Waldon, Redding CA, USA
Prophetic Teacher and Pastor
Pastor, Bethel Church, Redding

Miracles Beyond the Crowd by Nico Smit is a timely and compelling exploration of authentic faith. With clarity and conviction, Nico challenges readers to consider whether they are willing to rise above the noise, press beyond the crowd, and trust Jesus without compromise.

This book reminds us that mountains do not respond to religious language or casual faith, but to hearts aligned with the purposes of God. Through vivid illustrations and biblical insight, Nico reveals that sometimes the miracle begins not with us, but with those who carry us when we have no strength of our own.

More than stories of healing, *Miracles Beyond the Crowd* calls us to the greater miracle—a transformed heart that lives with eternal purpose. Inspiring, thought-provoking, and deeply rooted in Scripture, this book invites every believer to pursue a vibrant faith and to encounter Jesus, the true miracle worker.

Bernhard Wewege, New Zealand
Pastor and Prophetic Voice
Founder and Senior Leader, Every Nation Christchurch
CoFounder of Envisage Now

Pastor Nico Smit's *Miracles Beyond the Crowd* is a book of golden nuggets on every page and a deeply stirring call to authentic discipleship in an age of distraction and compromise. The book boldly declares that "the crowd will rarely lead you to Jesus—it will often lead you away."

Through powerful biblical insight, Nico exposes how modern culture's resistance to surrender mirrors the lukewarm spirit of Laodicea, where faith has become shaped more by the masses than by the Messiah.

Drawing from the Gospels—especially Mark's vivid portrayal of the crowd—Nico reminds readers that miracles come not to spectators but to seekers: those who "tear through rooftops" and "press through when the path is blocked." His retelling of Zacchaeus' encounter with Jesus captures the scandalous grace that transforms not only a man's heart but his home. Grace, Nico boldly argues, is shocking precisely because it meets us before we've proven ourselves worthy.

With clarity and conviction, *Miracles Beyond the Crowd* challenges believers to stop drifting with culture and instead "keep up with Jesus." It's a book that confronts complacency, rekindles hunger for God's presence, and invites every reader to exchange the applause of the crowd for the nearness of Christ. A timely and transforming read.

Clive Pawson, Perth WA, Australia
Pastor, Leader and Prophetic Minister
Lead Pastor at Christian Revival Church (Perth)

Pastor Nico's book is for every believer ready to move beyond the crowd and into the miraculous and the supernatural healing ministry. Drawing on powerful biblical examples, great insight and the rhema word, this message beautifully articulates the crucial truth: faith is not passive; it's a persistent pursuit.

It masterfully unpacks the difference between a curious crowd and a desperate, believing heart—the kind that Jesus always stops for. This book is a bold and practical call to action, equipping you and empowering you to walk this journey of faith and embrace the healing and miracles God intends for your life. It's a must-read for anyone who refuses to stay seated on the sidelines. It's for anyone ready to see miracles.

Ps Nico is a good friend, and his teaching will inspire you to walk and enjoy the manifestation of your miracle.

Alejandro Arias, Orlando FL, USA
Evangelist, Author and Pastor
President of AAIM Ministries International
Continental Director of Pentecost26
Great Gospel International

Foreword

"Now faith is the substance of things hoped for, the evidence of things not seen." (Hebrews 11: 1)

One of my favorite quotes from *Miracles Beyond the Crowd* is this: "It is scandalous what grace can do in a life surrendered to God!"

If faith is the evidence of things we believe and hope for -things we can't see – then our faith will be made visible in the things we do. Our willing surrender to our good Father is evidence of our faith. Our daily surrender is a continuation of that first moment of yielding in response to the love of Jesus Christ. Every decision we make and every action we take is evidence of our trust in our Creator. No matter where we find ourselves, whether at home, at work, on the sports field or in the car, what we do, how we think and what we say reflects our faith and trust. Faith changes the way we move. Surrender affects our way of being in the world.

Faith in a God who loves us unconditionally and sacrificially inspires the same love in us – our love for Jesus transforms the way we love others. We move towards suffering, instead of away from it. We bring hope and love to despair and fear, and we bring our faith when our friends struggle to find theirs.

Our surrender to the King who embraces the shunned, the unclean and the outcasts changes how we welcome and who we invite to sit at our tables. Jesus ignored the crowd and moved closer, compelled only by love. The crowd was usually surprised, sometimes repelled and often scandalized by the actions of their Savior.

In a world increasingly shaped by noise, distraction, and spiritual indifference, *Miracles Beyond the Crowd* offers a piercing and prophetic call to return to the heart of faith—a faith that moves, presses in, and refuses to settle for proximity without encounter.

Nico Smit's words are not merely reflections; they are invitations. Invitations to climb higher, to break through barriers, to reach for Jesus with a hunger that defies the crowd's comfort.

This book reveals a facet of the Father's heart you may not have encountered before. The pages of this book serve as a guide for anyone who is weary of remaining in one place. It speaks to the wounded, the waiting, the weary, and the wildly persistent.

With biblical insight through vivid storytelling, and raw honesty, Nico reminds us that miracles are not reserved for the elite or the perfect—they are found by those who dare to reach, climb, and cry out.

Whether you are in a season of pressing through, standing at a gate of loss, or simply longing for deeper intimacy with Jesus, this book will stir your spirit. It will challenge your assumptions, confront your comfort, and awaken your faith. And most of all, it will point you to the One who still walks among the crowds, stopping for the ones who choose to move toward Him.

As you dive into *Miracles Beyond the Crowd*, prepare to be moved. Prepare to be changed. And above all, prepare to encounter the miraculous—beyond the crowd

Tony Thompson, Atlanta GA, USA
Pastor, Author and International Speaker
Apostolic Leader of Glory City Network USA
Senior Pastor at Glory City Church Atlanta
Founder of Tony Thompson Ministries

PROLOGUE

Giving up is easy to do!

Remaining steadfast in faith is hard!

Don't follow the crowd, follow the Lord. Following Jesus is a choice that comes with corresponding actions of pursuit and faithFULLness!

Faith often calls for the serious ones to press beyond mere casual wishing into a place of complete conviction. Many people like the idea of coming to Jesus as an option but not many are prepared to back it with the kind of action that confirms they believe Jesus is the ONLY option. Could the crowd be the refiner?

Crowds are mentioned over one hundred times in the Gospels. Investigate these and you will soon discover their unintentional role as refiners, challengers and revealers of faith. They are like modern giants standing in the way of those wanting to take hold of God's promises. Crowds can set a mood for faith, or they can encourage an attitude of doubt. Crowds can cheer a person on, or they can despise and ridicule them. Crowds can block people or open up opportunities for them. Crowds are a part of life. Jesus often withdrew from the crowd…and so should you! Whenever they surrounded Jesus, He decided whether He was going to engage with them, navigate them, ignore them or overcome them. We can learn a lot about how Jesus stood out from the crowd. We can also learn a lot from those in the Gospels who found a crowd between them and the thing they were believing God for.

This book is for those still waiting in faith, listening in faith, looking in faith and praying in faith. It is for those willing to follow in faith even when the road ahead is difficult, blocked or unclear.

It's for the hungry. The searching. The persistent.

It's for the believing believer.

It is for those who recognize resistance, problems and obstacles, but refuse to allow or accept that anything can stand in the way or be bigger than Jesus.

This book is the end result of a series of sermons I preached in my local church on finding Jesus in the crowd. It was like God wanted me to bring the church to a place of deeper persistence, unwavering commitment and passionate worship. I believe that by bringing those messages into this book, every reader can experience the same miracles, breakthroughs, transformations, opportunities and encounters that the church experienced when it was preached.

A word of caution though. Applying these biblical principles might offend your religion and make your personal opinions worthless. It may require you to surrender every excuse, opinion and comfort that conforms you to the crowd. My hope is this: that in this book you will find something beyond the crowd – something that will be so much more valuable than anything you gave up to find it.

When you press into what God has already poured out for you, you unlock the overflow that's been waiting for you!

Introduction

THE ONES WHO KEPT WALKING

There is something sacred and beautiful about the ones who choose to not stop at the sight of a crowd. They may not always be seen. Their names are often not known or forgotten. Their faces are frequently overlooked. Their deeply real and painful stories are so easily buried beneath the noise of the crowd. But Heaven watches closely when someone, wounded and worn, chooses to keep walking.

Not everyone does.

The crowd gathers for many reasons. Some come to observe. Others arrive curious or skeptical. Many are content to stay in the back, caught between interest and unbelief. They press in not to pursue, but mostly just to watch. Some may even touch Jesus by accident. Not because they were reaching for Him, but because they came so very close.

Every now and then, there is one who chooses to press through with raw hunger and faith. There is something different about such a person. They've become tired of standing in the same place. They are done with waiting for something to change. Their need is greater than their fear, so they move. They may have been told they are disqualified and unwanted. They may have carried shame longer than anyone knows. But they have a deep stirring that says: reach anyway!

Heaven responds to that kind of faith!

FAITH GOES AFTER JESUS! We often imagine Jesus healing anyone who asked, as if He moved from town to town waving His hand over the sick and casting blessings like seeds in the wind. The truth carries more weight and more wonder. His miracles were often not random. They were deliberate, set in motion by somebody who decided to passionately pursue Him. Maybe you've never seen this before, but there is a reason so many of His healings happened not in the place where people stood, but in the place to where they followed Him.

Derek Prince once captured this reality with piercing insight:

"I think most of us picture Jesus going around just healing somebody here and healing somebody there, and somebody comes up to Him and says, 'Heal me,' and He heals them. Now occasionally He did that. But basically, He didn't. What He did was to choose a time and a place, get everybody who wanted healing there, and do the job from beginning to end at that one place and time. And in many, many cases He required the people to follow Him several days before He ministered to their physical needs.

I used to think how is it that Jesus had so many people that had so much faith. You know why? One reason was the unbelievers had dropped out long ago. Think if you were lame or blind or paralyzed and you had to walk twenty or thirty miles for two or three days before the Lord would minister to you. If you didn't have faith you wouldn't be there. I'll give you just some clear examples. In Matthew 12:15. But when Jesus knew it, He withdrew from there [wherever there was]. And great multitudes followed Him, and He healed them all.

Whom did He heal? But what had they done first? They followed Him. Not where they were. Do you understand? They had to move out from where they were to an unknown destination following Him until He chose to stop and start ministering healing."

(Quote by Derek Prince from the audio message, "Healing: The Message and Method of Jesus.")

Those words strip away the false comforts of a passive gospel. They leave no space for a faith that watches and waits from a safe distance.

The ones who were healed were not standing still. They *followed*. They left familiar places and stepped into uncertainty with nothing but trust. Their belief had substance, and it carried them onward.

This kind of faith is hard to explain. A quiet clarity and determination comes to us in those moments, when faith is no longer theory but inspired movement. When belief is no longer passive but a personal pursuit. When someone who should have given up decides to go one step further.

Faith has always been more than words. It shows up in the decisions we make when the answer is still unseen. It takes shape in the steps taken before the outcome is guaranteed or even clear. True faith carries weight because it walks. It does not require applause. It does not wait for consensus. It knows who Jesus is and moves accordingly. Trust inspires movement. Something happens then, something God does not ignore.

Rarely does such faith arise in the midst of a crowd. Crowds are good at watching. They are skilled at commentary. They can easily be provoked and manipulated. But healing rarely meets the ones who remain motionless in the middle of the multitude. It finds the ones who pursue, those who endure the journey, and those who stretch their faith beyond the reach of their strength.

Jesus did not overlook the crowd. He walked among them. He taught them. He loved them. Yet time and again, the Gospels show Him stopping for the ones in amongst the crowd who decided in their own hearts to intentionally reach for Him. Not because the crowd was undeserving, but because so few in it were willing to move in that way.

There is a cost to moving when others remain still. It draws attention. It stirs opinions. Some will question your motives, and others will dismiss your urgency. But anyone who has ever received something sacred will tell you that what they gained in His presence far outweighs the risk it took getting there.

This journey is not for the polished. It is for the hungry. It's for the ones who have tried everything else but still believe there is something more. The ones who are not content to stay close to truth without ever touching it. The ones who have decided that if Jesus can still be found, they will not stay behind.

Some come for the noise. Others come for the Name.

The difference is everything. Never forget it.

A Prophetic Word

In a vision recently, God showed me a picture of my wife and I walking up to a very nice-looking restaurant, but there was a big crowd standing around the door. It was blocked. Someone said to us, "You will never get in there!" Then we heard a voice from inside saying, "Bring them in. They're the owners' children."

Then I saw us sitting at a very fancy table with gold cutlery, all white plates, and white napkins. There was a brown leather folder in front of us, like a menu. I opened it to the middle only to see both sides were completely blank. I said, "I don't know what to order!" The voice said again, "This is your dad's place. You can order anything you want, and I'll bring it to you!" As those words were spoken, I saw a feather pen and it started writing things I had been praying about. Line by line answers to my prayer requests were written. Then the voice spoke again, "Can I recommend these! Your Father says they're good."

Then I received a WORD that I want to share with you. I heard God say:

"You must come and sit at My table. Get out from the crowd, the noise, the distractions, the constant cursing, the negativity and come and sit at My table. Don't worry about those looking through the window. This meal is yours. I'm honoring My word to you. I prepared this table for you, and you get to write the menu.

You are my beloved child, and I am so pleased with you. You left your old life to follow Me to places you had no idea I would take you. You trusted Me when I didn't tell you everything about the places you were going, what it would cost, or what you needed to do.

You trusted Me when what I asked of you made no sense and stirred up difficulty for you among your brothers and friends. Now, remember that I also said I would make you into a great nation, and I would bless you; I will make your name great, and you will be a blessing.

I will bless those who bless you, and whoever curses you I will curse; and all peoples on earth will be blessed through you. And I will keep My word. Well done, good and faithful one. Now build Me an altar here and worship Me. Enjoy this moment. The food is about to come out, and giants are on the menu. Feast and enjoy!"

For those reading this, I pray today you will take a seat at the Father's table because it's your Father's pleasure to bless you!

I encourage you to bring before God the dreams that burn brightest in your heart—the ones you almost don't dare to say out loud. Pray them boldly. Seek His heart for them. And remember the promises He has spoken over your life.

God's promises are not fragile. They are not limited by circumstance, nor are they dependent on the approval of the crowd. You will have to guard them, because there will be moments when opposition rises from the very crowd that seems to surround Jesus.

The room where the miracle is happening is often in sight, but you feel unable to get in. The noise, the opinions, the distractions, and even well-meaning people can create a barrier between you and what God has prepared for you. Sometimes the hardest place to get to is the place where God is already working. If you have faith and a promise from the Lord, don't let the crowd stop you. They haven't promised you anything.

Just like the paralytic man and his four friends in Mark chapter 2, the crowd blocking the door is not the final word. When the way seems blocked, pray, ask; God has another way. That way will often require faith that refuses to give up, faith that climbs higher, faith that is willing to get its hands dirty.

You may have promises from God that feel delayed because the door seems shut. You may be tempted to think the opportunity has passed you by. But if the Lord has spoken, the blessing is still inside. The question is, will you stop at the crowd, or will you find another way into His presence?

Sometimes you just need to change the crowd you're with. Your breakthrough may depend on surrounding yourself with people who will carry you in prayer, speak life when you want to quit, and refuse to stop short of the miracle.

And remember—when they lowered the paralytic man into the presence of Jesus, the first thing He gave was not the healing they expected, but the forgiveness they needed. Sometimes God answers our prayers in a way that reaches deeper than we imagined. He makes us new from the inside out.

Your blessing is waiting inside. If the door is blocked, go in through the roof. Your miracle and future are waiting for you inside. Get to Jesus today. Don't let the crowd and their doubts stop you from going in and enjoying what your Heavenly Father has prepared for you.

1

Faith And The Making Of Miracles

You can always tell when someone has real faith, not because they say the right things or carry a certain tone when they pray, but because there's movement in them. A quiet resolve. A walk that doesn't match the terrain. Something in them stretches, even when everything says DON'T. They move before they see. They speak before there is evidence. They step out when standing, waiting and backing off would be so much easier.

Somewhere deep inside, they know. They may not be able to explain it, but their posture says it all:

God said it, so I'm going!

That's faith in action.

The letter to the Hebrews describes it like this: "*Now faith is the substance of things hoped for, the evidence of things not seen*" (Hebrews 11:1). It's not theory or wishful thinking. It's the invisible thread that holds someone together when everything around them is falling apart. It reaches beyond where logic stops. It believes when no one else will. It builds when there are no tools and waits when there's no timeline.

It looks ahead and sees what others can't. Not because the road is clear, but because the promise is trusted.

Enter the crowd.

Many in the Bible knew what it felt like to be surrounded by doubt and uncertainty. The crowd is always full of voices. Voices that say it's too late. That the door is shut. That you're not the kind of person God would stop for. But when faith comes alive in someone, those voices lose their grip.

The comments of the crowd become unconvincing and powerless. Something rises up in you and moves forward anyway.

> *It reaches beyond where logic stops. It believes when no one else will.*

Consider the story of the woman with the issue of blood. She had been bleeding for twelve years.

Not for a day or a week or a season, but *twelve years*. She had lived through over four thousand mornings wrapped in pain and shame, every one of them marked by the same slow, relentless suffering. The bleeding wasn't just physical. It drained her dignity. It cost her relationships. It isolated her in every way a person can be cut off...spiritually, socially, emotionally, and financially.

She had gone to every physician she could find. One after another, they took her money and gave her nothing in return. Their remedies failed. Their solutions were feeble. Their promises faded. Instead of getting better, she only grew worse. Her condition was defining. She wasn't known by her name anymore, she was known by her issue. Her problem became her identity. Her uncontrollable suffering became her shame.

According to the law, she was unclean. That meant no touching. No embracing. No sitting where others sat. No entering the temple. No laying hands on her children or brushing her hand against a friend's shoulder in the marketplace. Anyone she touched became defiled by association. She was untouchable, bringing emotional pain on top of the physical problems she was facing.

Shame lives long when there's no interruption. But that day, something broke into her routine of despair. Word had reached her of a Man named Jesus. A Healer. A Rabbi. A Miracle Worker. She had heard what He did for others—the leper cleansed by a single word, the lame walking, the blind seeing. And though she had not seen Him herself, something inside her began to burn.

She thought, *If He could do that for them… maybe…*

As she started to dream in faith somewhere deep in her spirit, a conviction formed. She said to herself, not once, but over and over again, *If I can just touch the hem of His garment, I will be healed.*

Not His hand. Not His face. Not His attention. Just the hem. The very edge of His robe. That would be enough.

But there was a crowd.

There is *always* a crowd.

The streets were packed. People were pressing from every side. Jesus had arrived in town, and everyone wanted a glimpse of Him. They wanted to hear Him, to see what He might do, maybe even catch a miracle themselves. She was not the only one there that day with hope. She was the only one with nothing left to lose. Her desperation had become too much to bear. *If Jesus could help and heal others ... maybe He can help and heal me!*

She didn't wait to be called forward. She didn't wave to get His attention. She dropped to the ground and started crawling through the crowd that rejected her. Every step forward was through feet and robes and dust. Nobody noticed her. If they had, they might have rebuked her or drawn back in disgust. But she didn't care. Her focus had narrowed to one thing: *reach Him... touch His garment!*

She came up behind Him, close enough now to stretch out her hand. Her fingers brushed the fringe of His garment, and in that moment, something holy happened.

Her bleeding stopped.

The flow that had ruined her life for over a decade dried up in an instant. It didn't fade. It didn't slowly subside. It ceased *immediately*.

She felt it in her body. She knew she was healed. But she wasn't the only one who noticed.

Jesus Himself stopped walking. He turned in the middle of the moving crowd and asked the question that startled everyone: *"Who touched Me?"*

His disciples were baffled. The people were pressing in from every side. Dozens had brushed against Him. Everyone was touching Him. He had felt power leave His body. He had felt faith pull something from Heaven into Earth. Someone had touched Him with intention and confidence.

She tried to disappear. She had received what she came for. She wasn't looking to be seen or heard. But Jesus kept looking. Not out of anger. Not to shame her. He wanted her to know that the Healer wasn't just available—He was personal.

Trembling, she came forward. She fell at His feet and told Him everything.

Jesus looked at her...not with disgust, not with distance, but with the full weight of dignity, and He called her something no one else had in years:

"*Daughter.*"

Then He said, "*Your faith has made you well. Go in peace and be healed of your affliction.*"

In that moment, He gave her more than a cure. He gave her restoration. She was whole.

What left the doctors confused and the community condemning had been no match for one act of faith; faith that crawled when walking wasn't allowed, that reached when everything said stay back, that believed when every voice said give up.

She hadn't touched Him by accident. She had touched Him with faith and Heaven had answered. Faith doesn't wait for the miracle to be delivered to the door. It moves toward it, often through resistance.

Her crawl of faith through the crowd did not go unnoticed. Jesus might not have seen her approach and reach out in faith, but Heaven did. Every step she took God saw and drew near. Heaven was ready to answer her persistent crawl with *dunamis* power the moment her faith touched Jesus.

> *Faith doesn't wait for the miracle to be delivered...it moves toward it, often through resistance*

It would be easier if miracles came wrapped in comfort. If healing showed up on demand. If the answer always landed at our feet. But most of the time, breakthrough comes after a stretch. The stories that stand out in God's Word are the ones where someone dared to step outside of what was allowed, what was easy, or what was expected.

That kind of movement is what James was talking about when he wrote, *"Faith by itself, if it does not have works, is dead"* (James 2:17). Not because faith is earned through effort, but because real trust cannot stay motionless. Something shifts in the hands. In the feet. In the decisions. Belief becomes action. Conviction becomes pursuit.

There's a reason so many people were near Jesus but never received anything from Him. Crowds followed Him. Multitudes surrounded Him. But it wasn't the crowd that drew His power, it was the one who refused to stay silent, the one who refused to wait their turn, the one who reached in desperation and belief.

Bartimaeus was another desperately believing one. He was sitting where he always sat, on the edge of movement, but never part of it.

The road out of Jericho was busy that day. The noise was different. There was talk of Jesus coming through. A crowd had gathered, and they weren't walking quietly. Feet shuffled. Voices rose. Hopes were stirred. Someone said the Miracle Worker was near, and suddenly the dust was alive with anticipation.

Bartimaeus couldn't see it. He had never seen anything. His world had been wrapped in darkness from the beginning. No faces, no color, no shapes, just sound and scent and the constant ache of being left out. His name meant "son of honor," but life had treated him like anything but. He was a beggar. A man defined by lack. His place was on the roadside, wrapped in a cloak, dependent on the pity of passersby. He didn't know what it felt like to be chosen or chased or celebrated.

But he knew how to listen.

So, when the noise shifted, he noticed.

Voices said it was Jesus. Not just a rabbi. Not just a healer. *The* Jesus. The one who had opened blind eyes before. The one who cast out demons. The one who touched lepers and raised the dead. The one who spoke with authority and silenced storms.

He had heard enough stories to fuel the question: *Could this be my moment? Is this where I finally receive my sight?*

He couldn't see Jesus, but he could shout.

"Jesus, Son of David, have mercy on me!"

The words weren't impressive or eloquent, but they carried something that cut through the noise.

The people around him certainly heard. The crowd around Jesus heard, and they were not impressed. You must know crowds are rarely amused by or patient with bold faith. They love protocol, rules and cultural order.

"*Be quiet*," they snapped.

They didn't tell him gently. They rebuked him. They tried to push him back into place, to remind him who he was...blind, broken, and insignificant. They deemed him not worthy of the Rabbi's time, not part of the plan, and not worth interrupting the moment.

But he refused to be silenced. He cried out again, louder this time.

"Son of David, have mercy on me!"

No one gave him a mic. No one cleared a path. But that second cry—bold, raw, desperate—rose above the thousands. And Jesus stopped walking.

He didn't pause. He stopped.

The crowd kept moving. The conversations didn't end. But Jesus stood still and said, *"Call him."*

Bartimaeus didn't wait to be coaxed. He didn't demand proof. The moment he heard that Jesus was asking for him, he did something radical.

He threw off his cloak.

That piece of fabric may have looked insignificant to others, but it meant everything to him. That cloak identified him as a beggar. It validated his condition and gave him a legal right to his position in society. It was his survival. His identity. His fallback plan. If things didn't work out, he could always sit back down and beg again.

But faith doesn't carry a backup option.

So, he threw it off.

He rose, blind but burning with belief, and stumbled over to Jesus. Still no healing. Still no sight. But the miracle had already begun.

Jesus asked him a question that, on the surface, might have seemed unnecessary: *"What do you want Me to do for you?"*

He could have asked for money. He could have asked for help. He could have asked for a blessing or a better spot to sit.

But Bartimaeus didn't want temporary relief. He wanted transformation.

"Rabboni," he said, *"that I may receive my sight."*

Not Lord. Not Master. *Rabboni.* A personal term. A title of reverence and intimacy. It was the same word Mary Magdalene would later use when she recognized the risen Jesus. Bartimaeus wasn't asking a religious figure to perform a service. He was speaking to the One he knew could make him whole.

Jesus looked at him—not through him, not past him, but *at* him—and said, *"Go your way; your faith has made you well."*

Immediately, Bartimaeus could see.

The first face he ever saw was the face of Jesus. How glorious is that? The first thing he sees after he is made whole is Jesus, the ONE who did it.

An important thing to notice here is that he didn't go back to the road. He didn't return to the place he had been left in for so long.

Scripture says he followed Jesus along the way.

The healing didn't just restore his sight. It redirected his steps.

What started with a cry became a call. What began in darkness ended in discipleship. Bartimaeus received his miracle. Not because he had power, position, or permission, but because he had a faith that refused to sit still.

Not every pursuit is clean. Sometimes faith stumbles. Sometimes it's bruised. Sometimes it cries through gritted teeth. But it keeps moving!

The friends who carried the paralyzed man in Mark 2 understood this. They got to the door and found it blocked by people. Most would've taken that as a sign to try again later. But they had come too far to walk away now. So, they climbed. They tore the roof open. They interrupted the moment because they believed something greater was possible.

When Jesus saw the man being lowered down, He saw their faith.

Not their theology. Not their prayers. Their *faith*. Take note of that truth.

Miracles are seldom random acts of divine impulse. They are often precise responses to a kind of pursuit that refuses to back down. They don't reward the ones who wait politely in the background. They reward the ones who hear and know God's word and take the required action. Jesus didn't call everyone who believed in Him by name, but He always responded to those who stepped toward Him.

Some of those steps were loud. Some were quiet. Some looked like shouting, some looked like kneeling, others looked like climbing trees or falling at His feet. But all of them had one thing in common: they did not wait for the moment to come to them. They stepped toward it. They took that leap of faith and embraced the miracle Jesus was offering them.

Faith doesn't require certainty, but it does require surrender. It requires enough trust to move when logic says stay, to give when it seems foolish, and to keep praying when nothing has changed.

It doesn't always feel strong. Often, it's trembling, but it keeps going. Not because the path is clear, but because the One who called is trustworthy.

The ones who kept walking—the ones who cried out, tore roofs, pushed through crowds—those are the ones whose stories are still being told. They remind us that miracles are revealed to those who reach.

FAITH FOR MIRACLES

Faith rises from within the one who refuses to settle. It grows in the places where comfort is no longer an option and where clarity has not yet come. It lives in motion—not in rushing ahead, but in moving forward, step by step, even when the answer has not yet arrived. Faith takes root when someone begins to lean not on their own understanding, but on the voice of God that calls them further.

Faith speaks through decisions more than declarations. It reveals itself in the courage to keep walking, even with unanswered questions. It does not demand a blueprint before building. It does not hold back until all the pieces make sense. It follows with trust when there is nothing visible to follow.

Some try to reduce faith to a formula, but it refuses to be held that way. It carries the texture of lived experience, of tears on the floor, of long nights followed by a whispered yes. The woman who pressed through the crowd carried that kind of faith. So did Bartimaeus, shouting above the noise. Their belief reached beyond conditions and protocol. Neither of them had position, status, or invitation, but both found Jesus responding with power and compassion.

That kind of pursuit never gets ignored.

As for miracles, no one can schedule them, but it is possible to reach for them. Miracles are wrapped in God's mystery and purpose, but faith has access to them. When Jesus turned to the woman and said, "Your faith has made you well," He named what had drawn healing from Him—not the environment, not the attention of the crowd, but a decision she made in secret before she ever touched Him.

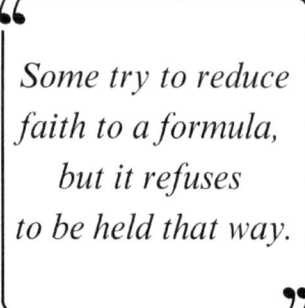

Some try to reduce faith to a formula, but it refuses to be held that way.

Miracles unfold when something in a person dares to act on what God has already made true. That action may come as a cry, a crawl, a shout, or a single silent stretch, but it comes.

A miracle is not simply a fix or a flash of power. It's the collision between divine authority and human surrender. Something in Heaven moves when a heart on earth continues to believe and won't back down.

There will always be many who stay seated—curious, respectful, and cautious. But the ones who receive are often the ones who refuse to stay where they've always been.

So, if the path ahead still looks uncertain but something within you keeps leaning forward, trust that movement. That's where faith begins. Not in the absence of risk, but in the refusal to remain still.

That's where the miraculous becomes possible.

2

Rip Open The Roof!

Capernaum was packed that day. Word had gotten out that Jesus was back in town. The house He entered couldn't contain the flood of people who came to see Him. Every door frame was filled. Every corner crammed. The crowd pressed in so tightly that not even one more body could squeeze through. And yet, four men arrived carrying someone who couldn't walk on his own.

They weren't looking for a sermon. They weren't there to listen. They were there for a miracle.

Their friend had been paralyzed for who knows how long. His legs didn't work. His condition had rendered him dependent, possibly even discarded by those who saw his life as no longer useful. But these four refused to let that be the end of the story. They picked him up, and they did so with determination and purpose.

Why? Because they knew Jesus was the only One who could change everything. They had faith!

When they reached the house, the crowd blocked every way in. There was no path to the door. No open window. No space to wiggle through. Many would have taken that as a sign to wait for another day.

To come back later. To pray from the outside and hope it would be enough.

But true faith has never, and should never, bow to inconvenience. Instead of backing off, they looked up.

In ancient Galilean homes, stairs often led to a flat roof made of mud, branches, and tiles. These friends didn't wait for permission or ask if this was acceptable. They climbed. With a grown man on a mat, they scaled that house. Then they started digging.

They didn't politely knock. They broke through.

They peeled away layers of roof until the hole was big enough to lower their friend down. Dust would have fallen into the room. Bits of debris would have hit people's heads and shoulders. The crowd inside may have gasped or backed away. But Jesus stood and watched as the man was lowered to His feet.

It's easy to imagine the tension in the room. All eyes were on Jesus, waiting for His response. Would He be annoyed? Offended? Would He rebuke them for interrupting His message?

Mark records what happened next with clarity: "*When Jesus saw their faith, He said to the paralytic, 'Son, your sins are forgiven'*" (Mark 2:5).

Notice the shift. The faith He saw was not the paralyzed man's, but his friends'. It was their action, their refusal to stop, their determination to bring their friend into the presence of Jesus that opened the heavens.

Jesus didn't comment on their passion or their teamwork. He saw faith. Not belief locked away in hearts, but faith made visible in movement.

Before He healed the man's body, He touched something deeper. He forgave his sins. The man came for physical restoration, but Jesus first offered spiritual redemption. That's how He always works. From the inside out. The external miracle is often the echo of something far greater He has already begun deep on the inside.

But not everyone in the room celebrated. Some scribes were sitting nearby, silent in speech but loud in judgment. They questioned in their hearts, "Who can forgive sins but God alone?"

> *Not belief locked away in hearts, but faith made visible in movement*

Jesus, knowing their thoughts, addressed them directly. "Which is easier," He asked, "to say to the paralytic, 'Your sins are forgiven,' or to say, 'Rise, take up your bed and walk'?"

Then He continued, *"But that you may know that the Son of Man has authority on earth to forgive sins..."* and He turned to the man and said, *"I say to you, rise, pick up your bed, and go home."*

And he did.

The man who had arrived on a mat carried by others now walked out carrying the mat himself. No longer defined by his weakness. No longer waiting outside the flow of life. He walked out in full view of everyone, healed from the inside out.

The room was left in awe. Can you even imagine that scene?

Some miracles are easy to celebrate because they cost nothing. But this one disrupted the whole environment. It required risk. Labor. A decision to act boldly and publicly.

That's what faith looks like when it's lived.

Sometimes, your miracle doesn't begin with you. It begins with the people who carry you when you've run out of strength. Friends who don't wait for conditions to improve. People who drag you up the stairs, tear through whatever's blocking the way, and place you before the only One who can restore what's broken.

Those kinds of friends are rare. They don't settle. They don't retreat. They rip open the roof if they have to. And the moment Jesus sees that kind of faith—faith that climbs, faith that carries, faith that refuses to let a barrier win—something happens. He moves. He heals. He forgives.

Breakthrough may not come through the front door. The crowd might always be in the way. But roofs aren't off-limits. Not when you know the One who's inside.

Too many people have friends that will carry them away from Jesus when they actually need friends who will carry them to JESUS! This is why your circle matters. The crowd you are in matters. Who you walk with will often determine how far you go. If you are surrounded by people who stop at the crowd, you'll stop at the crowd. If your closest companions shrink back when it gets hard, your faith will shrink back too. But if your friends know how to climb when the way is blocked, you'll find yourself on a rooftop with a miracle waiting below.

Think of it this way: every one of us have moments when our faith runs thin, when our strength feels gone, and when discouragement presses heavy on our shoulders. In those moments, you need people who will not only pray for you but who will *carry you*. People who will hold you up when you can't hold yourself. Friends who will take you into the presence of Jesus even if it means inconvenience, embarrassment, or risk. When you have friends like that, faith will never be out of your reach.

Now, let's turn the question around. What kind of friend are you? Are you willing to climb a roof for someone else's miracle? Are you willing to carry another's burden, to intercede until breakthrough comes, to refuse to give up on someone even when they've given up on themselves? The greatest friendships in the Kingdom are forged in costly love.

The paralytic never asked his friends to break open a roof. He didn't give them instructions or a strategy. But they acted because they believed. Sometimes the strongest thing you can do for someone you love is to have faith on their behalf when they cannot summon it for themselves. That is Kingdom friendship - faith that fights for another.

It is also worth noticing that Jesus did not only see *the paralyzed man's faith*. The Bible says, *"When Jesus saw **their** faith..."* It was a collective faith, shared among the four who carried and the one who was carried. Your faith is never only your own. It impacts the people around you, and their faith strengthens yours.

Together, we rise. Together, we reach roofs. Together, we see God move.

So, ask yourself: Who are the people you let closest to your heart? Are they faith-carriers or doubt-spreaders? Are they roof-tearers or crowd-settlers? And when your turn comes, because it always does, will you be found among those who stop at the door or those who climb higher to bring life into impossible places?

BEYOND THE CROWD

Have you ever felt completely alone in the middle of a crowd?

People bustling all around you, laughter and conversation filling the air, yet not a single soul actually sees you? It happens more than we admit. In rooms full of movement and noise, hearts still ache with isolation.

But when God looks at a crowd, He never sees a mass. He sees individuals. You are never reduced to a number in His sight. He sees the person. He knows every story, every reason someone came. And when someone presses into what He's freely made available, they receive what others only observe.

The crowd will rarely lead you to Jesus. It will often lead you away.

Culture isn't growing more committed to Christ. It grows more resistant to surrender. When the way requires sacrifice, the crowd veers off. That's why following Jesus can never be about keeping up with culture. What we need to be focusing on is keeping up with Jesus!

> *What matters most is not what the crowd is doing ... but what Jesus is doing*

What matters most is not what the crowd is doing or where it's heading, but what Jesus is doing. Where is He going? What is He saying? What is He drawing you into?

When Jesus addressed the church in Laodicea in Revelation 3:16, His words were blunt: *"You are lukewarm... I will spit you out."* Laodicea comes from the Greek root *laos*, meaning "a crowd" or "mass of common people." It wasn't simply a cold-hearted city; it was a spiritually indifferent one, shaped more by the masses than by the Messiah.

You won't find miracles by floating along. The crowd often blocks the way or pulls you off course. And any space you leave between you and Jesus will not remain empty for long. The crowd will fill it. Distraction will fill it. Culture, voices, fears, and fatigue will flood in unless you actively press forward.

Miracles don't happen accidentally. They follow those who refuse to stand still. Those who tear through rooftops, cry louder when silenced, or press through when the path is blocked.

Mark's Gospel makes something clear: the crowd is a character. The crowd is mentioned thirty-three times in that one Gospel. It watched Jesus. It followed Jesus. It also rejected Him and screamed, "Crucify Him!" Crowds are fickle. They may cheer on Sunday and curse by Friday.

You have to choose your direction carefully. Paul wrote to the Philippians, saying, "*I forget what lies behind and strain toward what lies ahead. I press toward the goal for the prize of the upward call of God in Christ Jesus*" (Philippians 3:13–14). The direction of your life is shaped by the decisions you make every day - toward God or toward the world. Each step takes you closer to one and further from the other.

Paul gave everything—his breath, his strength, his entire life—as an offering to the One who saved him. He wouldn't put anything ahead of God. To betray the call placed on his life would have been unthinkable.

The obstacle between you and the presence of God is not Him. It's your willingness to reach for what He has already promised.

Not long ago, I hiked up to a place behind our city known as "The Lost World." The hike was exhausting. It was steep, hot, and harder than expected. But when I finally reached the top, what I saw was unforgettable. The view was overwhelming in the best way. And that's often the case with the most beautiful things in life. The journey isn't always comfortable. The road isn't always clear. Sometimes it's not until the very end that you understand why it was worth it.

That's why so many give up before they see the promise.

They look at the climb and judge the destination. They choose ease over endurance. They shout at the mountain instead of prophesying to it. But the ones who trust the Promise-Maker, keeping their eyes fixed on His promise, those are the ones who walk in the beauty of its fulfillment.

Don't trade the promises of God for a life of comfort. Don't overvalue the size of your challenge and undervalue the weight of His Word. The addiction to carnal ways will always drag your heart away from the freedom found in total surrender. But if God spoke something over your life, He meant it.

Press in. Lean forward. Stretch your faith. God remains faithful!

If what you see is all you believe, then faith is missing. Faith takes hold of what's unseen and pulls it fully into this present visible reality.

Jesus was constantly surrounded by people. The crowds followed Him everywhere. Some cheered. Some crushed. Some later condemned. But the ones who truly reached Him were the ones who stepped beyond the crowd. It was never a competition, but it did require courage. The ones who pushed through, who touched Him with faith, those were the ones He stopped for.

Deep choices introduce miracle moments.

If you don't believe there's a miracle waiting beyond the crowd, you'll have no reason to keep moving. But when you believe Jesus still heals, when you believe no crowd is thick enough to stop His power, you push forward with conviction.

Moses sent twelve spies into the promised land. All of them saw the same obstacles. Only Joshua and Caleb saw through the eyes of faith. The rest judged the promise by the challenge. But faith presses through what looks like walls and walks into what God already said was yours.

Not every mountain moves when you speak to it. Some shift because you believe they will.

In Matthew 17:20, Jesus said something that many have quoted but few have lived: *"If you have faith as a mustard seed, you will say to this mountain, 'Move from here to there,' and it will move; and nothing will be impossible for you."* He was teaching them to speak what God had already made true. The size of the seed wasn't the focus: the trust behind the voice was.

> *Not every mountain moves when you speak to it. Some shift because you believe they will*

Mountains do not respond to religious language or casual faith. They respond to conviction, agreement with the heart of God, and to someone who has already settled the question of who He is and what He can do.

That's where the miracle begins.

Jesus said, *"From the days of John the Baptist until now, the Kingdom of Heaven suffers violence, and the violent take it by force"* (Matthew 11:12).

Faith may shout or it may whisper, but either way, it grabs hold and refuses to let go.

Bill Johnson once said, "Whether faith cries out very loudly or it quietly strengthens people to press forward, faith-actions always seem violent in the spirit world. Faith grabs hold of an invisible, superior reality, and it won't let go."

Too many never see what God could have done in their lives because they followed the flow. They let culture decide their pace. They stayed close enough to the crowd to feel safe but never close enough to Jesus to be changed.

Be different. Set a new course. Trust Him.

The world will always offer a safer way, a quieter life, a more popular path. But miracles live beyond the crowd.

After all... would you rather blend in, or be someone Jesus stops for?

Rip through your limitations. Get beyond the crowd!

He is still available.
He is still accessible.
And He is still incredible!

3

When The Table Feeds The Uninvited

Jesus withdrew to the region of Tyre and Sidon - gentile territory. The move wasn't random. He wasn't retreating, but He wasn't staying in familiar places either. Some theologians suggest He went there to rest, away from the pressure of crowds and constant confrontation with religious leaders. Yet even outside the borders of Israel, He couldn't stay hidden.

She heard He was nearby.

She wasn't Jewish. She wasn't religious by their standards. She had no heritage, no pedigree, no entitlement to the promises of God. But she had a need, and it was a desperate one. Her daughter was tormented by a demon, and no one else could help her. She came, crying out: *"Have mercy on me, Lord, Son of David! My daughter is severely oppressed by a demon!"*

She knew the titles. She used language that showed understanding, maybe more understanding than those who had seen His miracles firsthand. She called Him Son of David, the messianic name. She recognized who He was before the miracle happened.

But He answered her with silence. Not a word. No nod. No glance. Nothing.

Most people walk away after being ignored once. Silence has a way of sending a message. But she didn't leave. She kept crying out, so persistently that the disciples finally asked Jesus to send her away. She was being rejected by the ones who were supposed to represent Him.

Still, she stayed.

Jesus finally turned and spoke. *"I was sent only to the lost sheep of Israel."*

His words didn't sound welcoming. He made it clear that her name wasn't on the guest list. The promises weren't for her. She was outside the covenant.

But instead of turning back, she stepped closer. She knelt before Him and said, *"Lord, help me."*

He responded again, this time with a phrase that might offend even the most faithful heart.

"It is not right to take the children's bread and toss it to the dogs."

Ouch. The words hit hard. In Jewish culture, gentiles were often referred to as dogs...unclean, outside, and unworthy. Some try to soften it by pointing out the word used was for a household pet, not a street scavenger. But either way, it was clear: *she didn't belong at the table.*

But her humility ran deeper than her hurt.

"Yes, Lord," she replied, *"but even the dogs eat the crumbs that fall from their master's table."*

That response did what nothing else had. It stopped Him.

She didn't argue. She didn't protest. She didn't demand to be included. She simply believed that even the smallest leftover from His table held more than enough power to transform her life. She didn't ask for the feast. She asked for the *overflow*.

And He looked at her with a kind of joy He rarely expressed.

"Woman, great is your faith! Let it be done for you as you desire."

In that very hour, her daughter was healed.

> He called her faith **great**. This woman came as an outsider and left with a miracle.

There's something powerful about a person who doesn't walk away when the answer takes too long. She didn't shut down after being ignored. She didn't lose heart after being dismissed. She wasn't undone by the insult. She kept coming. She kept worshiping. She kept believing.

She changed the conversation. In a moment where everything told her she didn't belong, she remained. She didn't demand status. Instead, she reached for grace, and in doing so, she accessed something others had taken for granted.

Jesus didn't say that about many people. He often marveled at unbelief, but this time He celebrated the exact opposite. He called her faith *great*.

This woman came as an outsider and left with a miracle. Her daughter was restored, her faith affirmed, and her legacy recorded. Not because she had the right background or qualifications, but because she wouldn't give up.

Her story still speaks to us today. Many stop short in the moment when silence stretches too long or when the first "no" lands heavy. Many recoil when the answer doesn't match their expectation. But those who stay in the tension, who keep kneeling, keep asking, keep believing, even when every sign says, "not now", those are the ones who find more than they came for.

She believed in the abundance of Jesus so deeply that even a crumb would suffice, and she wasn't wrong.

FEASTING ON CRUMBS

I'm hungry enough to take the crumbs, even if all that's left is the tiniest morsel. But have you ever considered that compassion, true, desperate compassion, can look scandalous? Imagine finding yourself near a wild animal's nest like a plover or magpie. At the slightest threat to her young, the mother screams, rises up, and risks everything. Her only thought is, *protect my babies.*

That's how the Canaanite woman behaved. Her daughter was demon-possessed. She knew evil was loose in her home, threatening her family. Rather than walk away from Jesus because she belonged to the "wrong" crowd, or didn't fit the promise, she leaned in. She cried out: "*Lord, have mercy. Help me. I'll take crumbs.*"

She crossed every line of culture and religion to believe crumbs from Jesus were still powerful enough to set her child free. She didn't wait for permission. She refused to be silenced by tradition or put down by murmurs. She wasn't demanding a seat at the table, she was merely asking for a crumb. Yet in that proclamation, Jesus saw her heart. He called out her astonishingly persistent faith and healed her daughter instantly.

Let's face it: the disciples thought her cry was annoying. They tried to send her away, but she refused to leave until she heard the mercy of God. She humbly accepted being called a "little dog," even though that status in Hebrew culture stood for the unclean, the outsiders. But she pressed in anyway, not offended but firmly believing that even the leftovers on the master's table were enough to reverse a nightmare in her home.

Historically, she was a Canaanite—an ethnic identity with social and economic stigma. Yet Jesus called her to Himself. He turned traditions upside down and showed that mercy isn't reserved for insiders. It's for the broken, desperate, bold-hearted ones who won't take a "no" as the final answer.

Faith needs mustard-seed resolve. Even crumbs have power. Jesus once fed thousands from five loaves, and leftovers filled baskets. He did that to show that there is always enough, whether that be enough bread, enough blessing, or enough restoration.

When she spoke her faith in the face of disgrace, she released supernatural authority. She didn't bring her daughter forward. She said, "*Lord, help me*." She believed God's healing power could move across distance, beyond ceremony. And it did. Her house was transformed without Jesus stepping foot inside.

Her story is a call to all of us. If our theology has become tidy and comfortable, we miss miracles. If we rely more on protocol than persistence, we overlook power. If we shrink from the outspoken, daring, unconventional faith she exercised, we shrink from revival.

She didn't command her daughter healed. She declared faith and let God do the work. That kind of faith - tenacious, untamed, and undeterred, is contagious.

This woman offered a scandalous act of worship in the face of cultural exclusion, and Jesus turned that moment into a legacy that echoes into eternity.

> *If we rely more on protocol than persistence, we overlook power*

What obstacle does your situation seem to say is bigger than God?
Who is blocking your way to faith?
What ceiling of belief needs tearing off in your life?
Can you be humble enough to ask for a crumb, while determined to stay until it becomes a feast?

You can't scare God with your faith. He is never startled by honesty, persistence, or audacity. He welcomes the vulnerable, the outsider, and the bold. His table is open. His blessing is ample. His compassion is scandalous.

So, reach again. Ask. Believe. Persist. Eventually, the crumb becomes the restoration of your house, and your soul.

WHEN ISSUES BECOME IDENTITY

There are moments when the things we carry begin to carry us. Wounds that were once temporary start to shape how we see the world, how we speak, and even how we believe. Over time, pain takes root so deeply that it becomes part of the way we think about ourselves. Struggles linger so long they begin to answer to our name. And the longer those issues remain unresolved, the more likely they are to be mistaken for identity.

In the Bible, people are often introduced not by their names, but by the duration or nature of their struggle. It's as if the issue becomes the headline of their lives. What once happened *to* them becomes the thing that defines them.

Many carry wounds like that—hidden, unspoken burdens that have stretched far beyond the moment of injury. They might not be visible, but they are real. Some began in childhood. Others were caused by betrayal, loss, trauma, or fear. Some are physical, others emotional or spiritual, but all carry weight. Whether it's been months or years, too many have begun to believe that the pain will always be part of the story.

It doesn't have to be.

There is no wound so old that Jesus cannot heal it. There is no issue so rooted that His power cannot uproot it. But healing rarely comes passively. It comes when faith decides to move forward.

Throughout the Gospels, we see people healed in two ways—either Jesus touches them, or they reach out to touch Him. Both required faith. But the latter required initiative. The kind of initiative that grows when desperation gives birth to boldness. That kind of faith doesn't wait for a perfect moment. It moves toward hope even when the way forward isn't clear.

That's often the dividing line. Some wait for healing to find them, others pursue it. And the ones who pursue it usually do so not because they're stronger, but because they've come to the end of everything else.

Issues that go unaddressed begin to reshape every part of life. They strain relationships, color expectations, and drain spiritual vitality. Long-term pain can silence joy. It can convince us that things will never change, that miracles are for others, and that we've somehow missed our moment. But nothing in the kingdom of God is ever too far gone for restoration.

It's important to recognize that we don't overcome these things by minimizing them or pretending they don't exist. Healing begins when we acknowledge the pain and carry it to Jesus. It begins with a decision to stop hiding, stop pretending, and stop excusing. It begins with an honest step toward the only One who can actually make us whole.

Both required faith. But the latter required initiative.

Faith does not deny the presence of an issue, it simply refuses to let the issue have the final word.

Some wounds are deep enough to require more than time. They require a holy touch. And the longer the wound has lasted, the more intentional we must be about bringing it to the Lord. Otherwise, it will quietly become a filter through which we see everything—God, people, even ourselves.

There comes a point when talking about the problem is no longer enough. There comes a point when we need to shift from conversation to transformation, from rehearsing what's broken to reaching for the One who restores.

The enemy would love for you to believe that your issue is permanent. He would love to keep you convinced that nothing will ever change. But the moment you turn to Jesus and reach in faith, even with trembling hands and a weary heart, things begin to shift.

Sometimes the healing begins with a whisper of belief: *"If I can just get to Him..."*

Not every breakthrough is loud. Some start in the quiet places, in the corners of worship, in the back rows of churches, or alone in a car where no one else is watching. But in those moments, when your heart leans toward Him with expectancy, He sees. He knows. And He responds.

There is a difference between hoping Jesus might do something and believing He already wants to. The first waits for a miracle. The second moves toward one.

Issues often carry shame. But Jesus does not recoil from the unclean. He does not turn away from those whose lives have unraveled. He isn't worried about catching what we carry. On the contrary, everything unclean that touches Him becomes clean. Everything broken finds healing. Everyone overlooked is seen.

No one is disqualified from receiving what Jesus so freely gives.

He still heals. He still restores. And the invitation to reach out in faith is still open. Whether your struggle has lasted twelve years or twelve days, whether it's recent or deeply rooted, the answer remains the same - come to Him. Reach with your heart, speak with your faith, and believe that what He has done before, He can do again.

You may feel uninvited or unworthy, but remember this: Nothing is beyond His reach, and no one is beyond His love.

A striking example comes from the pool of Bethesda in John 5:1–15. The scene unfolds in Jerusalem, near the Sheep Gate, where a pool with five colonnades had become known as a gathering place for the desperate. John describes it as crowded with people who were blind, lame, and paralyzed, each waiting for something to change, each carrying their own silent pain. Among them was a man who had been there for thirty-eight years. We are not told his name, his background, or even his family story. He is introduced only by his condition: "an invalid for thirty-eight years." His identity had been swallowed up by his issue.

Think about the length of that timeline. Thirty-eight years. That is nearly four decades of waiting. Long enough for the issue to no longer feel like an interruption, but a definition. Long enough for it to shape how others viewed him and how he viewed himself. In the eyes of those who passed by, he was not an individual with dreams, dignity, or destiny, he was the man who couldn't move. The years of waiting had reduced him to a condition, a headline that announced his struggle before he could say a word.

Day after day, his world revolved around the waters of Bethesda. Local belief held that an angel would occasionally stir the waters, and the first of the whole crowd to step in would be the only one healed. There was faith, but not in God. The pool, with its promise of relief, became both a place of hope and a place of extreme disappointment. Every ripple in the water sparked a race for deliverance which this man could never win. Each missed moment must have deepened the wound of hopelessness. Each year that passed without change must have reinforced the idea that this was simply who he was now. His mat was more than a place to lie down; it became his identity card, the emblem of a life confined and defined by limitation.

Then Jesus entered the scene. Walking through the crowd of people the Gospel tells us that He saw the man lying there and knew how long he had been in that condition. Imagine that...Jesus not only saw him among so many but understood the depth of his personal story. Others may have glanced and moved on, but Jesus stopped. And His first words are striking: *"Do you want to get well?"* or maybe He could also have said: *"Do you want to get out of here?"* On the surface, it sounds almost absurd. Of course he wanted healing and freedom from that place. Why else would he linger at the pool? But Jesus was not asking about a shallow desire. He was probing deeper, reaching into the very core of the man's identity. After thirty-eight years being in a crowd of brokenness, it is possible to become so accustomed to brokenness that we no longer know who we would be without it. The crowd was his people. It is possible to cling to the familiarity of pain because it becomes such a big part of who we are.

> *Jesus was probing deeper, reaching into the very core of the man's identity.*

The man's answer revealed his mindset: *"I have no one to help me into the pool when the water is stirred. While I am trying to get in, someone else goes down ahead of me."* He was in the crowd, but he was alone. His hope was tied to others, and his excuses were tied to the system around him. He explained why healing had not come, but he missed the fact that Healing Himself was standing before him. Isn't that often the way with us? We can get so fixated on the way we think God has to move that we overlook the new way He is already moving.

Jesus did not entertain the excuses or affirm the superstition about the waters. He cut through all of it with one clear command: *"Get up! Pick up your mat and walk."* No stirring of water, no angelic sign, no waiting for the right timing. Just a word. And the Gospel says, *"At once the man was cured; he picked up his mat and walked."* After thirty-eight years of paralysis, muscles strengthened, nerves reconnected, and legs carried him forward. In a single moment, his story was rewritten.

Notice the detail: he picked up his mat and walked out on the crowd. For decades that mat had carried him in that place. It was the place of his weakness, the surface of his shame. But now, by the command of Jesus, the very thing that symbolized his limitation became a testimony of his liberation. He carried what once carried him. The issue that defined his identity was no longer the headline of his life. He was no longer "the man who had been an invalid." He became a living testimony that issues, no matter how long-standing, do not have the final word when Jesus steps in.

There is a powerful lesson here. Sometimes issues linger for so long that they start to feel permanent. The man at the pool had likely resigned himself to the thought that nothing would ever change. The pool and the crowd that gathered there had become his whole world. But Jesus proved that no matter how many years pain had stayed, His word is stronger. What once looked like a dead end became a doorway into new life. His healing was a restoration of dignity, identity, and hope.

This story is a reminder to anyone who has lived under the shadow of a long struggle. Your mat does not define you. Your years of waiting do not disqualify you. The crowd with the same issues does not define you. Your identity is not chained to your issue. The same Jesus who spoke at Bethesda still speaks today. He does not ask you to explain the past or justify the wait. He asks you to believe that a different future is possible. His word is enough to raise you, restore you, and give you back what you thought was lost forever.

The Pool of Bethesda itself carried deep cultural and religious meaning. Archaeologists have uncovered its remains in Jerusalem, near the Sheep Gate, confirming the biblical account. What they found was not one simple pond, but a large complex of two pools surrounded by five covered colonnades. In the first century, this space would have been bustling with crowds of sick and desperate men and women who gathered daily with the same fragile hope: that perhaps today would be the day something changed.

The belief that healing could come from the pool reflected both Jewish and Greco-Roman influences of the time. In Jewish tradition, water often carried sacred significance. Ritual baths, or *mikva'ot*, were used for purification. Flowing water symbolized cleansing, renewal, and access to God's presence. At the same time, Greco-Roman culture embraced the idea of healing springs, where gods like Asclepius were believed to bring restoration. The pool of Bethesda sat at the intersection of these religious ideas, becoming a place where people merged superstition with desperate faith.

John tells us that people believed an angel would stir the waters. Some manuscripts add that the first one in after the stirring would be healed. Whether this was legend, tradition, or a distorted mixture of hopes, the result was the same: crowds of broken people waited, staring at ripples, convinced that their breakthrough depended on beating everyone else into the water. The pool became a theater of competition, where the weakest were most disadvantaged. For someone like the paralyzed man, unable to move quickly and dependent on others, it was a place of daily humiliation. Every splash that he couldn't reach must have reminded him of his inability, reinforcing the lie that healing was for others, but not for him.

What makes Jesus' act so radical is that He completely bypassed their religious system. He didn't wait for water to move or for the religious people to give Him permission. He didn't ask the man to crawl or compete. He didn't affirm or argue the superstition of the place. Instead, He declared healing with a word, proving that His authority was not bound to pools, rituals, or traditions. In essence, He was saying: "You don't need the water. You need Me."

For the Jewish leaders, this moment carried even more weight. Jesus performed the miracle on the Sabbath. To them, healing and carrying a mat on that day violated the law. But Jesus was making a larger statement: the God who created the Sabbath was standing in their midst, bringing the true rest the Sabbath pointed toward. The pool could offer hope once in a while, for the first who got in. But Jesus offered healing to anyone who would believe.

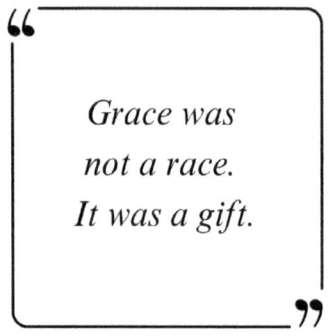

> Grace was not a race. It was a gift.

Understanding this cultural backdrop deepens the story's power. The pool of Bethesda was a place where human hope collided with human helplessness, where superstition mingled with longing, and where competition left many in despair. Into that very setting, Jesus stepped, not to affirm the broken system, but to show a better way. His presence declared that God was not distant, nor was healing a prize for the fastest or strongest. Grace was not a race. It was a gift.

This means something for us today. We may not be lying beside a literal pool, but how often do we find ourselves waiting at our own "Bethesda"? Waiting for the right set of circumstances, the right people, the right timing, believing that if everything aligns, then healing or breakthrough will finally be possible. But Jesus comes to us in those very places of waiting and says, "Do you want to be made well? Then look to Me." He is not bound to the systems we depend on. He is not limited by the delays we've endured, and He does not require us to win the race to receive His grace.

4

Open The Door For Jesus

Jericho was buzzing with curiosity when Jesus came through town, more than usual, because rumor had it He might pass that way again. Among the crowd stood Zacchaeus, a man with a reputation that preceded him. He collected taxes for Rome, a universal symbol of betrayal among his own people. He lived off others' hardship and profited from their oppression. There was nothing humanly admirable about him. For most, he was an example of what not to be.

But there was a hunger in him still that money couldn't satisfy. A longing for something true. When he heard Jesus was coming, Zacchaeus made a choice that startled everyone around him: he climbed up a sycamore tree.

Several things stood out that day:

CLIMB HIGHER

Zacchaeus was too short to see Jesus over the crowd; too reviled to be invited forward and too compromised to belong. Yet something stirred inside him. He still believed he could see. He still thought maybe Jesus would bring something new into his life. So, he climbed.

In a crowd where reputations ruin hope, he climbed higher. He risked exposure. He risked embarrassment. But he risked faith more than fear.

From below, Jesus looked up, paused mid-step, and called him by name: "*Zacchaeus, hurry and come down; for today I must stay at your house.*"

The passing comment spoke volumes, not about Zacchaeus' standing in the city, but about what Jesus saw in his heart. That invitation was radical. Jesus didn't follow the rules. He invited Himself to Zacchaeus' home. He crossed every cultural, moral, and religious barrier to do it.

The crowd around them gasped, probably in disapproval. But something greater was happening.

Because Jesus came to stay, the next thing Zacchaeus did was the only thing that made sense. He stood and said, "*Look, Lord, I give half my possessions to the poor; and if I have defrauded anyone, I restore it fourfold.*"

What a turn! This was not a man only bent on healing or comfort. He was repentant. He was willing to restore. He responded to revelation with radical obedience.

Then Jesus declared: "*Today salvation has come to this house, because he also is a son of Abraham. For the Son of Man has come to seek and to save the lost.*"

A standing tax collector, known as a thief by society, became a redeemed son of faith because he climbed above the noise. He took initiative. He risked being seen. He let Jesus into his home, and his life changed forever.

Reputation and history don't define revelation. Zacchaeus lived under a name that was synonymous with betrayal. As a chief tax collector, he wasn't simply disliked, he was despised. To his fellow Jews, he was a traitor who had sold himself to Rome, enriching himself by draining his neighbors. His history screamed corruption, and his reputation shut every door of belonging. Yet, in the middle of all the anger surrounding him, Jesus saw past the labels. He looked beyond what Zacchaeus had done to who Zacchaeus was made to be. That moment reminds us that grace doesn't stop at the boundaries of public opinion. The Gospel breaks through reputations that seem beyond repair.

Sometimes you must rise above the noise to see clearly. The crowd had already written Zacchaeus off. To them, his story was finished before it even began. They decided he had no place in God's kingdom and no seat at Jesus's table. Yet Zacchaeus refused to let their verdict be

...grace doesn't stop at the boundaries of public opinion.

the last word. He climbed a sycamore tree, lifting himself above the voices that tried to drown him out. From that higher perspective, he could see Jesus more clearly than those who mocked him. What the crowd tried to keep him from, his determination led him into. Zacchaeus shows us something timeless in that act: sometimes faith looks like climbing, like refusing to stay where others have left you, like doing whatever it takes to catch a glimpse of the One who can rewrite your story.

INTIMACY FOLLOWS INITIATIVE

Zacchaeus didn't wait for Jesus to find him in his house. He didn't demand that Jesus come into his space. He made the first move, pressing past shame and climbing toward possibility. That small but bold act positioned him for something far greater than he imagined. When Jesus reached that spot, He looked up, called Zacchaeus by name, and invited Himself over. A man who had been shut out by the crowd suddenly found himself welcomed by the Savior. It all began with a step—a climb that no one else was willing to make. Intimacy with Jesus often unfolds in the lives of those willing to move toward Him before anyone else does.

> *Jesus didn't come to reprimand Zacchaeus. He came to redeem him.*

And notice this: Jesus didn't come to reprimand Zacchaeus. He came to redeem him. While the crowd waited for condemnation, Jesus extended communion. While they muttered about his sin, Jesus offered him salvation. In the space of one meal, everything changed. Zacchaeus opened his home, but more importantly, he opened his heart. He pledged to repay what he had stolen and to give generously to the poor. A man known for taking became a man who gave. And what had been a life defined by greed was now defined by grace. Because Jesus stayed, Zacchaeus surrendered. And because Zacchaeus surrendered, restoration followed.

The story leaves us with questions we cannot ignore: Have you ever felt too small to matter, too notorious to be saved, or too stuck to reach out? What voices from the crowd still echo in your mind, telling you that you are disqualified from hope? And where do you need to climb above the distractions—the shame, the noise, the limitations—to catch a clearer view of Jesus?

Zacchaeus teaches us this: it's never too late or too far gone when you're hungry for redemption. What matters is your willingness to see more than the crowd. To climb above the limitations. To reach for something real.

Jesus actively looks for hearts that are still searching, even in the mess. He invites Himself. He stays with you. And salvation begins not with finding Him, but with Him finding you.

Take the risk. Climb, even if others shake their heads. He will call your name. And when He does, salvation it will come home with you.

WHEN JESUS REDEFINES THE HOUSE

Zacchaeus' name meant "righteous," yet his life had been anything but. Short in stature and, by many accounts, short in character, he still had one quality that made all the difference: he wanted to see Jesus badly enough to do something about it. When the crowd blocked his view, he climbed a sycamore tree. It was hardly dignified for a wealthy, powerful man, but dignity mattered less than his hunger to encounter Christ.

Jesus was surrounded by people almost everywhere He went, but He had a way of noticing the one in the crowd who was truly reaching for Him. This time, He stopped beneath that tree, looked up, and called Zacchaeus by name. It wasn't a casual greeting. It was personal. It was intentional, and it came with a startling declaration: *"I MUST stay at your house today."*

That "must" was divine necessity. Jesus was not content to leave Zacchaeus up in a tree, seeing Him from a distance. He wanted to step into Zacchaeus' real life, behind the walls where the truth lived. The crowd only saw a corrupt tax collector who had profited by cheating his own people. Jesus saw a man who was lost but ready to be found.

This was the kind of turnaround Jesus had just said was *"impossible with man but possible with God"* (Luke 18:27). The crowd muttered in disbelief, but Jesus knew exactly what had taken place. *"Today salvation has come to this house,"* He said, making it clear that the change was the evidence of a heart set free.

Zacchaeus' story challenges anyone content to encounter Jesus only in public, at a safe distance. Crowds are good at blocking views and muffling voices, but transformation rarely happens in the noise of the street. It happens when you welcome Him inside...into your space, your habits, your private world.

Jesus is still calling people down from their "trees" of safe observation. He is still saying, *"I MUST stay at your house."* The question is whether we will keep Him at the doorway or open the door wide and let Him come in, even if it means confronting what needs to change.

Zacchaeus thought the greatest obstacle to seeing Jesus was the crowd in front of him. In truth, the bigger obstacle was the house behind him. His home represented everything about his life: the wealth gained from unfair taxes, the status he built on exploitation, and the comfort he had secured while others struggled. That house was his fortress, but also his prison. To the crowd, his home was a monument of greed. Yet that's the very place Jesus chose to enter.

When Jesus said, "Today I MUST stay at your house," He wasn't simply asking for a meal. He was saying, *I want to step into the center of your life, the place that defines you most.* For Zacchaeus, that place was his home. For us, it might be our habits, our relationships, our patterns of thinking. Jesus doesn't only want access to the public side of our faith, the parts we're proud to show. He wants the house, the private space where our real selves live.

This invitation flips the script on religion. The crowd expected Jesus to dine with the righteous, to endorse the best homes and avoid the worst. But grace is never afraid of the mess. Jesus doesn't look for the cleanest house; He looks for the one most in need of transformation.

Notice, too, that Jesus said, *"I MUST."* It wasn't casual. It was divine appointment with urgency. Zacchaeus was right at the heart of God's plan. When Jesus chooses to enter someone's home, it is never accidental. He doesn't wander into places by mistake. Every invitation He gives is deliberate, full of purpose, and loaded with potential for transformation.

For Zacchaeus, opening the door meant exposing his reality. People knew he was wealthy, but they didn't know the details of how he lived. Letting Jesus in meant allowing the Lord to see the books, the possessions, the table where deals were made. That takes courage. It's one thing to shout "Hosanna" in a crowd; it's another to let the Savior sit at your dining table where every secret rests.

We can relate more than we admit. There are rooms in our lives that feel "off-limits" to God: the grudges we hold, the habits we excuse, and the thoughts we hide. But when Jesus enters, He doesn't want a tour of the tidy rooms; He wants the keys to the locked ones. Salvation doesn't happen at the doorway. It happens when He walks all the way in.

The irony is that Zacchaeus' house, once a symbol of exploitation, became a stage for restoration. In the same place where money had been mishandled, generosity now overflowed. In the same home where neighbors once feared being cheated, they now heard promises of repayment. That's how redemption works! It rewrites the story not somewhere else, but in the very place shame once lived.

This is why Jesus entering the house matters so deeply. Public miracles inspire, but private transformations endure. The crowd saw Zacchaeus climb, but his neighbors saw him change. And it all started because Jesus chose to redefine the meaning of that house.

We must ask ourselves: if Jesus said today, "I must stay at your house," would we open the door? Would we let Him into the places that feel too compromised, too messy, too painful? Or would we keep Him at the threshold, satisfied with admiration but afraid of intimacy?

The beauty of Zacchaeus' story is that he didn't hesitate. God's Word says he *"hurried down and welcomed Him gladly"* (Luke 19:6). What began as desperation to see Jesus became an eagerness to host Him. That's the pivot of salvation, when curiosity turns into surrender, and surrender turns into joy.

And here's the miracle: Zacchaeus' house itself gained a new identity. No longer a monument of corruption, it became a testimony of grace. No longer a place of secrecy, it became a place of salvation. Jesus had redefined it, and when He redefines a house, He redefines a life.

SCANDALOUS GRACE

When Jesus called Zacchaeus down from the sycamore tree and announced His intention to stay at his house, the reaction was immediate. Luke tells us, *"All the people saw this and began to mutter, 'He has gone to be the guest of a sinner'"* (Luke 19:7). The scandal wasn't that Zacchaeus had climbed a tree. It wasn't even that he had cheated his people for years. The real scandal, in the eyes of the crowd, was that Jesus, the holy teacher, the miracle worker, the one many hoped was the Messiah, would willingly sit down at the table of someone like Zacchaeus.

To them, holiness meant separation. Holiness was about distance from sin and sinners. For a rabbi to cross that boundary was shocking, even offensive. Why spend time with a traitor when there were so many more "deserving" people in Jericho? Why risk reputation on someone whose reputation was beyond repair? In their eyes, Jesus had undermined His credibility with one decision.

But that's always what grace looks like to those who believe righteousness must be earned. Grace is shocking. Grace is offensive. Grace looks unfair. The crowd wanted repentance first, then acceptance. They wanted Zacchaeus to prove himself worthy, to show some evidence of change, and to make restitution before he was welcomed. But Jesus reversed the order. He extended acceptance before Zacchaeus lifted a finger. He chose communion first, knowing that repentance would follow.

That is still how Jesus works today. Romans 5:8 reminds us that *"while we were still sinners, Christ died for us."* Grace does not wait for us to be ready. It does not wait for us to be respectable. It does not wait for us to prove ourselves. Grace shows up uninvited and undeserved, extending an open hand when we are still tangled in our failures.

> *He chose communion first, knowing that repentance would follow.*

For many modern readers, that's where the scandal of grace comes alive. Because if we're honest, there are people we secretly believe are beyond redemption. Their sins are too public, too scandalous, too offensive to us. Maybe it's the addict who has burned every bridge. Maybe it's the politician who abused power. Maybe it's the abuser, the criminal, or the person whose choices have left visible wreckage. Our instinct is often to close the door, to decide they're unfit for grace until they have proved otherwise.

But Jesus doesn't work that way. He didn't wait until Zacchaeus repaid the money to walk into his house. He didn't wait until he cleaned up his record or rebuilt his reputation. Jesus stepped across the threshold before the crowd ever saw change. And that's what offends us—grace moves ahead of our categories. Grace breaks the rules we've written for who belongs and who doesn't.

The modern church still struggles with this. We talk about being welcoming, but when someone truly broken, visibly messy, or morally compromised steps through the doors, our first reaction can mirror that crowd in Jericho. We mutter. We wonder. We hesitate. We silently question why God would waste His time on "someone like that." The scandal of grace is that Jesus keeps choosing "those people." He keeps stepping into the houses we'd rather avoid.

And here's the deeper truth: if we look closely, we're all Zacchaeus. Every one of us has lived off compromise, betrayal, or selfish gain at some point. Maybe our sins are more socially acceptable, but they're no less real. Pride, greed, gossip, lust, bitterness, envy...all of them make us outsiders to God's holiness. And yet Jesus calls us down from our own "trees" of distance. He looks up, says our name, and insists, "I MUST stay at your house today."

That's the heart of grace: Jesus comes while we are still unworthy. He chooses communion over condemnation. And when we encounter Him, the transformation begins. Notice that Zacchaeus didn't shrug off his past when grace came knocking. He didn't say, "Great, now I can keep living as before." No, grace awakened something deeper in him. He promised restitution far beyond what the law required. His heart shifted from greed to generosity, from taking to giving, from betrayal to restoration. The crowd didn't believe he could change, but grace made it possible.

It is scandalous what grace can do in a life surrendered to God! This is the pattern of grace we see over and over in Scripture. Think of the Samaritan woman at the well (John 4). Her reputation was ruined, her past tangled, her standing in the community shot. Yet Jesus engaged her, spoke to her, and revealed Himself as the Messiah. Grace went first, and repentance followed. Or consider the woman caught in adultery (John 8). The crowd wanted condemnation, but Jesus extended mercy: *"Neither do I condemn you. Go now and leave your life of sin."* Grace again preceded transformation.

For modern believers like us, this raises uncomfortable but necessary questions. Do we believe grace is still scandalous enough to welcome the undeserving? Do we extend acceptance to people before they've proven themselves? Or are we more like the muttering crowd, waiting for repentance before we're willing to open the door?

> *It is scandalous what grace can do in a life surrendered to God!*

The scandal of grace is not that God saves bad people. The scandal is that God saves people before they've stopped being bad. He doesn't endorse their sin; He transforms their hearts. But the order matters. He comes in first. He sits down first. He makes Himself at home first. That grace creates the space for everything else to change.

Perhaps this is why Jesus declared at the end of Zacchaeus' story, *"The Son of Man came to seek and to save the lost"* (Luke 19:10). Not the respectable. Not the already-repentant. Not the crowd-approved. The lost. And if that makes us uncomfortable, then maybe we've forgotten that's exactly what we were when He found us.

Behold, I stand at the door and knock. If anyone hears My voice and opens the door, I will come in to him and dine with him, and he with Me. (Revelation 3:20)

5

When Worship Breaks The Room

It happened in a small house in Bethany; the kind of moment that would live forever in the memory of heaven and be told everywhere the Gospel would go. Jesus was sitting at the table in the home of Simon the Leper. Around Him were the familiar sounds of conversation, laughter, and movement; people coming and going, the clink of dishes, and the low hum of voices. Then, without warning, the atmosphere shifted.

A woman walked into the room carrying an alabaster flask; beautiful, fragile, and sealed tight. Inside was *nard*—spikenard—an oil so rare it had to be harvested from plants growing more than 3,000 meters high in the Himalayas. It was thick, fragrant, and costly, worth a year's wages for the average worker. People used it sparingly, drop by drop, for special purposes: a touch in wine, a dab in perfume, a small amount to mask the scent of death at a funeral.

But she didn't come to use it sparingly. She came to *pour it out*.

Without asking permission, without reading the room, she broke the neck of the flask (no going back now) and poured the entire contents over His head. The thick perfume ran down His hair and onto His shoulders, saturating His clothes. The smell filled the house instantly, curling around every corner.

And that's when the voices started.

WHY THIS WASTE?

When the alabaster jar broke and the fragrance filled the house, it should have been a moment of unrestrained wonder. A woman, moved by love, desperation, gratitude, or perhaps all three, offered something so extravagant it left everyone stunned. Yet instead of celebrating the beauty of her act, the first sound recorded is criticism.

Matthew tells us the disciples were indignant, muttering among themselves that the perfume could have been sold for a high price and given to the poor (Matthew 26:8–9). Mark narrows it down further: "Some" began to scold her harshly, their tone sharp, their words cutting (Mark 14:4–5). John removes all vagueness: it was Judas who spoke up first, calculating the cost at three hundred denarii, nearly a year's wages (John 12:4–5). Three different Gospel perspectives, yet all circling the same refrain: *"Why this waste?"*

To the disciples, her act made no financial sense. The flask was sealed, meaning once it was broken there would be no reclaiming even a drop. Every ounce of that precious nard could have been measured, weighed, sold, redistributed, and accounted for. A good economist would call her foolish. A charitable leader might label her impulsive. To the practical mind, it was the height of bad stewardship.

But stewardship and worship are not always the same thing. The disciples saw expense; she saw opportunity. They saw numbers; she saw worth. What they considered wasted, Jesus called beautiful. That's because in God's kingdom, value is not measured by efficiency but by sacrifice. The currency of heaven has never been spreadsheets or balance sheets. It has always been hearts willing to pour out everything for love's sake.

> *...in God's kingdom, value is not measured by efficiency but by sacrifice.*

This is where the story pierces us. Because even today, every true worshiper eventually faces the same tension. Pour your energy, time, or resources into following Jesus wholeheartedly, and someone will call it waste. "You could have done something more productive." "You should have invested that elsewhere." "You're being too extreme." Whether it's your schedule, your generosity, or your devotion, expect that there will always be many voices ready to scold. This is what crowds do when they see such acts of intimacy.

Here, those voices come not from strangers but from disciples and friends. The disciples were not outsiders; they were the ones who had walked with Jesus for years, who had seen miracles firsthand, who knew His power and presence. Yet even they missed the meaning in this woman's act. Familiarity had dulled their sense of wonder. They had grown so used to Jesus being among them that they failed to recognize the significance of honoring Him in this moment.

The question "Why this waste?" exposes something deeper: what do we believe is *worth it*? To Judas, worth was measured in coins. To the disciples, worth was measured in social responsibility. To the woman, worth was measured in love. She didn't do the math because her heart had already been counted as His. And when the heart is consumed with love for Jesus, no offering is too much.

Think of how this applies in our modern world. Consider the person who commits to daily prayer when others see it as wasted time. Think of the believer who tithes faithfully or gives sacrificially while friends whisper that they could have used that money for something more practical. Think about the ones who see giving as an expression of love when their friends think only those compelled by law could be so generous. Consider the young man or woman who chooses purity in a culture that calls it foolish, or the family that leaves comfort behind to serve in a mission field while others shake their heads in confusion. Over and over again, devotion to Jesus is branded as "wasteful" by those who cannot see its worth.

But here is the secret: true worship has never been efficient. True worship has always been costly. David declared, "*I will not offer to the Lord my God that which costs me nothing*" (2 Samuel 24:24). That principle echoes through the centuries. Real devotion costs reputation. It costs dignity. It costs resources. It costs control. Worship that does not move us out of comfort into sacrifice is more performance than offering.

The disciples thought they were defending a noble cause, that of the poor. But John reveals the heart of Judas, who "*did not care about the poor but was a thief; as keeper of the money bag, he used to help himself to what was put into it*" (John 12:6). Judas cloaked greed in the language of charity, but Jesus saw straight through it. There will always be voices that disguise criticism as practicality, but practicality without love becomes cold. And love without cost becomes hollow.

> "Worship that does not move us out of comfort into sacrifice is more performance than offering."

Jesus' response cuts through the noise: *"Leave her alone. Why do you trouble her? She has done a beautiful thing to me"* (Mark 14:6). In one sentence, He redefines what beauty is. Not the efficiency of a transaction, but the extravagance of love. Not what makes sense on paper, but what makes heaven pause in wonder.

And then He added something astonishing: *"Wherever this gospel is preached in the whole world, what she has done will also be told, in memory of her"* (Mark 14:9). The disciples' words of criticism faded into history, but her act of worship became eternal. What they dismissed as waste, Jesus immortalized as legacy.

That is the paradox of true worship. To the world, it may look like waste. To Jesus, it is unforgettable. To the world, it may seem unreasonable. To Jesus, it is beautiful. The jar was shattered, the oil was gone, the fragrance lingered only for a while, yet the story still breathes across centuries because love poured out for Him is never wasted.

So, the question is not whether others will misunderstand your devotion. They will. The real question is: who are you trying to please, the muttering crowd or the Master who calls it beautiful?

THE TRUE COST OF OIL

Oil has always come at a price. To get olive oil, the olives must be crushed. To get spikenard, the plant must be harvested, crushed, and distilled. Precious oil is born out of pressure.

Our spiritual "oil" is no different. The anointing you carry, the depth of your worship, often comes through seasons of crushing, pressing, and breaking.

We read about Paul's anointing, but listen to his testimony in 2 Corinthians 11:

"Five times I received forty stripes minus one. Three times I was beaten with rods; once I was stoned; three times shipwrecked; a night and a day in the deep, in perils, in hunger, in thirst, in cold and nakedness, and besides everything else, my deep concern for all the churches."

That's oil talking. That's the cost behind the fragrance.

We live in a culture that wants the oil without the crushing, the power without the process. But every pressing season will produce something, either the sweet fragrance of worship or the bitter stench of resentment.

> *...she was pouring out more than perfume, she was pouring out her story.*

This woman's oil was costly because her life had been costly. She wasn't rich in the way the room assumed. She had been wounded by sin, marked by grief, and desperate for hope. Her jar wasn't filled by accident; it had been bought at great price, perhaps saved over years. When she broke it open for Jesus, she was pouring out more than perfume, she was pouring out her story.

YOU DON'T KNOW MY STORY

No one else in that room knew what it cost her to walk in there. They saw a woman with a jar, but they didn't see the woman who carried wounds that no jar could measure. They didn't know the nights she cried herself to sleep, replaying regrets that haunted her. They didn't know the betrayals that cut her so deeply she wondered if she could ever trust again. They didn't know the shame she endured from whispers and stares that followed her every step. They didn't know the crushing seasons when she thought her life was over, when survival itself felt like a miracle. They saw the alabaster flask, but they never saw the cost behind it.

The same is true for you! People might see you lift your hands in worship, but they don't know the valleys that shaped those hands. They don't know about the midnight prayers you prayed when no one else was listening. They don't know about the times you sat in silence because words failed you and all you had were tears. They don't know the storms that almost drowned you, the losses that stripped you bare, the nights you whispered, *"God, if You don't hold me, I won't make it."* They see your worship now, but they don't see the scars that gave birth to it.

That's why true worship cannot be measured by someone else's opinion. It is too personal, too costly, too sacred to be weighed on anyone else's scale. What you pour out on Jesus is not for them to evaluate, it's for Him alone. The disciples saw waste. The critics saw extravagance. But Jesus saw a story. He saw the pain behind the perfume, the surrender behind the fragrance, the brokenness that made the offering beautiful.

This is what makes worship powerful. It is not performance. It is testimony. Every tear that falls in His presence carries history. Every lifted hand is a story of survival. Every hallelujah sung through trembling lips is proof that the grave did not win. People see the glory of your worship, but they cannot imagine the hidden path that brought you here. *You don't know my story—all you see is God's glory.* (John P. Kee)

Think about Hannah in 1 Samuel 1. The priest Eli saw her lips moving in desperate prayer and thought she was drunk, but he didn't know her story. He didn't know the years of barrenness, the ache of unanswered prayers, the sting of Peninnah's mocking. To Eli, she looked foolish. To God, she looked faithful, and out of that misunderstood moment came Samuel, a prophet who would change Israel's future.

Or think of David dancing before the Lord with all his might as the ark of the covenant entered Jerusalem (2 Samuel 6). Michal, watching from the window, despised him in her heart. She thought his worship was undignified, excessive, embarrassing. But Michal didn't know David's story...how God pulled him from obscurity, delivered him from Saul's spear, and established him as king. David's response was simple: *"I will become even more undignified than this."* Because when you know what God has done for you, you stop caring about what others think.

> *This is what makes worship powerful. It is not performance. It is testimony.*

The truth is, no one fully understands the cost of another's worship. They weren't there when you wrestled in prayer for your children. They weren't with you in the hospital room when you begged God for healing. They didn't feel the loneliness of betrayal or the shame of failure. They didn't watch you get up again after falling, again and again, until finally grace lifted you higher than your weakness. They weren't there, but Jesus was. He has been present for every tear, every wound, every crushing blow. And that is why when you pour out your worship, He calls it beautiful.

Modern life doesn't change this reality. People may misunderstand why you spend hours in prayer when your to-do list is long. They may criticize why you give generously when you could be saving more. They may question why you prioritize worship when others choose leisure. They may whisper, *"Why this waste?"* But they don't know your story. They don't know the moments when God provided in ways that no paycheck could explain. They don't know the healing He worked in your heart when bitterness should have consumed you. They don't know the freedom you found in Christ after years of chains. Your worship doesn't belong to their commentary; it belongs to the God who wrote your story.

And that's the wonder of it: when you pour out your oil, the fragrance fills the room for everyone, but the meaning belongs to you and Jesus. What they smell as perfume, you know as survival. What they call excess, you know as gratitude. What they see as too much, you know as not enough for the One who saved you.

So, never let the criticism of crowds silence your worship. Never let their misunderstanding convince you to hold back. You don't owe them your story. You don't owe them your explanations. You owe Him your oil. And if your worship looks extravagant to them, let it be. Because only you and Jesus know the cost, and He says it is beautiful.

You don't know my story. All you see is God's glory. And that's the point: my scars tell His faithfulness, my wounds reveal His healing, and my worship declares His worth.

SHE DID WHAT SHE COULD

Jesus silenced the critics. His words cut through their murmurs like a blade: *"Leave her alone. Why are you bothering her? She has done a beautiful thing for me... She has done what she could. She poured perfume on my body beforehand to prepare for my burial."*

What a defense. What a declaration. In a room full of opinions and judgements where her offering was dismissed as waste, Jesus framed it as worship. In the presence of those who measured devotion by practicality, He measured it by sacrifice. And in front of those who missed the significance of the moment, He revealed that she was the only one who grasped it.

Think about it. Jesus had spoken of His death before. He had told His disciples plainly that He would be betrayed, arrested, crucified, and raised again. Yet even His closest friends failed to see what was coming. They argued about who would be greatest. They fought over positions at the table. But this woman, whether she fully understood or whether the Spirit stirred something deeper in her, acted as if she knew time was short. She moved as though she understood what others had missed.

Perfume in an alabaster jar was not reusable. Once the seal was broken, there was no putting it back. The fragrance would either be released in that moment or lost forever. She had one chance, one moment, one opportunity to pour it all out, and she took it.

That's why Jesus honored her. She didn't wait until the cross to offer what she carried. She didn't wait until after His death to weep over His body. She poured it out *beforehand*—in advance, when it mattered most, when the opportunity was still open. Timing in worship matters. There are moments in life when delay means loss, when hesitation means missing the very encounter your soul longs for. This woman seized her moment. She broke the jar. She poured it all. She gave while she could.

How many of us have missed opportunities because we waited for a "better time"? We thought, *I'll give when I have more. I'll serve when I feel stronger. I'll worship when things settle down. I'll pour my oil when it's more convenient.* But worship that waits for convenience rarely costs much. Worship that hesitates often evaporates. The alabaster jar won't stay sealed forever. The moment to give, to serve, to lift your voice, to step forward, it won't always come back around.

This is why Jesus' words pierce so deeply: *"She did what she could."* She didn't wait until she could do what others thought was enough. She didn't withhold because her act might seem small compared to others. She didn't measure her worship against the opinions in the room. She simply did what she could, and in God's kingdom, that was more than enough.

Too often we hold back because we think what we have isn't significant. We imagine that unless we can sing like others, give like others, preach like others, our offering won't matter. But the beauty of this story is that Jesus doesn't weigh worship by comparison. He doesn't say, *"She did what they could."* He says, *"She did what she could."* Heaven measures devotion not by what you don't have, but by what you do with what you've been given.

And notice, Jesus called her act preparation. *"She poured perfume on my body beforehand to prepare for my burial."* She may not have fully understood, but in her obedience, she participated in something eternal. Her worship reached beyond her own moment and into the divine plan of God. That's what happens when you give all you have: God multiplies the meaning. You think you're pouring oil on His head, but in reality, you are preparing the way for resurrection.

For modern readers like us, this is where the story presses us. What does it look like to "do what you can" right now? Maybe it means praying when you feel weak, giving when your resources feel small, singing when your heart feels heavy. Maybe it means serving someone else when your own schedule feels overwhelming. Maybe it means forgiving when bitterness seems easier. Whatever it is, the kingdom of God values the step you *can* take, not the one you can't.

Timing still matters. You may never get another chance to speak encouragement into someone's life. You may never have another opportunity to pray with your children the way you can today. You may not always have the strength you do right now to lift your hands in worship. You may not always have the voice to sing the song you've been holding back. The alabaster jar is in your hands, and the seal will not last forever. The fragrance must be released now, or it may be lost.

That's why the woman's act still echoes through history. She didn't wait until it was socially acceptable. She didn't wait until everyone understood. She didn't wait until the disciples approved. She poured it out then and there, and Jesus declared that her act would be remembered wherever the gospel was preached.

Your worship might not make sense to others. It might even feel foolish in the moment. But if you do what you can, if you pour it out while the opportunity is here, you will step into something eternal. The world may forget, but heaven will never forget.

So, what alabaster jar are you still holding sealed? What act of devotion have you been waiting to release until the "right time"? Don't wait for tomorrow. Don't wait for everyone's approval. Don't wait for life to calm down. Break the jar. Pour it out. Do what you can.

Because when you do, Jesus will say of you what He said of her: *"They have done a beautiful thing for me."*

It's important to notice something: her worship disrupted the room. People were offended. It broke their sense of propriety. It crossed their boundaries of what was "appropriate."

True worship often does that. It's not always neat, quiet, or predictable. Sometimes it breaks through decorum. Sometimes it rattles the people who think they're closest to Jesus. Sometimes it offends the religious mind while moving the heart of God.

David danced before the Lord with all his might, and Michal despised him for it. The woman in Luke 7 wept on Jesus' feet and dried them with her hair, and Simon the Pharisee judged her for it. In Bethany, she broke her jar, and the disciples rebuked her for it.

> **True worship ....Sometimes it offends the religious mind while moving the heart of God.**

The pattern is clear: if your worship never risks misunderstanding, you may not have poured out enough yet.

This woman's act leaves no room for half measures. You don't break an alabaster jar and then try to catch some back in the bottle. You don't pour out nard and hope to recover it later.

That's the nature of true worship, it's all or nothing. You bring your whole heart, your whole devotion, your whole offering. You don't hold some back in case it doesn't "work out."

David understood this. When offered a threshing floor for free to make an offering, he refused. *"I will not offer to the Lord my God that which costs me nothing"* (2 Samuel 24:24). That site would one day become the temple mount, a place where generations would worship. The cost you pay now can bless generations after you.

Mark says the house was filled with the fragrance. In the Greek, the word is *osmē*—used in Scripture to describe the pleasing aroma of worship or sacrifice to God. That night, Bethany became a sanctuary.

And Jesus Himself carried that fragrance. When He left that house, when He prayed in Gethsemane, when He stood before Pilate, when He carried the cross—the scent of that nard clung to Him. When the soldiers mocked Him, when the nails pierced His hands, the aroma of her devotion was still there. She had, without realizing it, anointed

Him for burial. That is what the scent of nard was used for... but did she know? God knew and she obeyed.

Think about that: the last act of love Jesus experienced before the cross was this woman's costly, poured-out worship.

HAVE YOU BROKEN THE JAR?

The alabaster jar was never meant to remain sealed, and neither is your worship. The question still presses against our hearts today: *Have you broken the jar?*

So many believers hold back, not because they don't love Jesus, but because they are waiting for the "perfect moment." They are saving their oil for a day that feels more convenient, for a season when life is less chaotic, for a setting where others will understand. But alabaster jars were not designed to sit on shelves forever. Their value was in their breaking. The fragrance locked inside could not bless anyone until the seal was shattered. Oil was made to be poured. Worship was made to be given. Love was made to be expressed without reservation.

And yet, how often do we guard what was meant to flow freely? We ration out devotion as if Jesus deserves only what is left over after everything else is satisfied. We calculate, we measure, we wonder what others will think. But real worship has always defied calculation. The woman with the alabaster jar didn't measure the cost against her reputation or against the disapproval in the room. She didn't think about resale value or long-term investment. She thought only of Jesus—His worth, His presence, His nearness. That focus freed her hands to break what others thought should be preserved.

Here is the challenge for every modern disciple: What alabaster jar are you keeping sealed? Maybe it's your time—you say you'll serve the Lord when life slows down, but life never does. Maybe it's your resources—you tell yourself you'll give when you feel more financially secure, but security never feels complete. Maybe it's your vulnerability—you hold back your worship in church because you don't want others to see your tears, your shouts, or your surrender. But the longer the jar stays sealed, the longer the fragrance stays trapped.

Breaking the jar always carries risk. It risks misunderstanding. It risks offense. Someone in the room will always think you've gone too far. In fact, if your worship has never caused discomfort for someone watching, it might not be costing you as much as you think. True devotion rarely looks "reasonable" to the world, or even to religious bystanders. But Jesus never rebuked the extravagance of love. He rebuked the hesitation of those who withheld.

When you break the jar, something happens that no one else can stop. The fragrance fills the room. It lingers. It marks everyone present—even those who complained. Worship is never wasted. What others call excessive, heaven calls beautiful. What others dismiss as emotional, Jesus treasures as eternal. When the jar is broken, your life becomes the vessel of a fragrance that rises beyond the walls of the room and reaches the very throne of God.

Think about it this way: the jar was fragile, but the fragrance was powerful. Your life is fragile too, but what God has placed within you—faith, love, testimony, anointing—was never meant to stay sealed up. It was meant to flow, to bless, to fill atmospheres with the presence of Jesus. You may feel small, breakable, or overlooked, but when your worship is poured out, it becomes something far greater than you.

So here is the question again, burning in the text and echoing across centuries: *Have you broken the jar?* Or are you still holding it close, waiting for a more convenient season? There will always be excuses, always be reasons to wait. There will always be a crowd telling you not now! But the truth is this: the longer you wait, the easier it becomes to keep waiting. Faith moves now. Worship acts today. Love expresses itself while the opportunity remains.

Yes, it may offend some. Yes, it may be misunderstood. But your oil was never meant for them. Your jar was never meant for their approval. Your worship is for Jesus alone. And when the seal finally breaks, the fragrance that rises will move His heart. That is the only audience that matters.

So, don't hold back. Don't wait for a better time. Don't let the alabaster jar sit unbroken on a shelf while days slip by. Lift it, break it, pour it out. For the King is in the room, and He is worthy of nothing less than everything.

6

Don't Die Before Your Time

D*on't let the crowd lead you to a funeral.*

The Bible makes it clear: how we live and what we believe can either lengthen or shorten our days.

- **2 Chronicles 16:12** tells of King Asa, who died before his time. Even with an exceedingly great disease, he refused to seek the Lord.
- **Ecclesiastes 8:13** warns, "The days of the wicked will not be prolonged."
- **Proverbs 10:27** promises that "the fear of the Lord prolongs life, but the years of the wicked are shortened."
- Twenty-five times, the Bible repeats the command to *honor your father and mother* so "your days on the earth may be long."
- In **Acts 5**, Ananias and Sapphira fell dead in the house of God—not because it was His will, but because they lied to the Holy Spirit.
- In **Job 1:12**, God set a boundary for Satan, refusing to give permission to shorten Job's life.

If it weren't possible to die before your time, God's Word wouldn't mention it so often.

Ecclesiastes 7:17 says it plainly: *"Do not be overly wicked, nor be foolish; why should you die before your time?"*

God wants you to live!

This is an urgent word for now: God's heart is for you to live fully, vibrantly, and abundantly. Jesus Himself said in John 10:10, *"I have come that they may have life, and have it to the full."* Yet many today are existing without truly living. The pressures of life choke out joy. Disappointments weigh down hope. The enemy whispers lies that convince people to settle for survival instead of pressing into abundance.

Some of us know that suffocating feeling all too well. Life has been drowned in disappointment, sabotaged by betrayal, or buried under relentless pressure. For some, the fire has gone out slowly, almost unnoticed—like a candle burning low until the flame disappears. For others, it feels like a sudden blow, a moment when the heart broke, the dream died, or the strength was stolen. Either way, the result is the same: people walking, talking, working, and moving through life, but no longer alive on the inside.

Pain has a way of making death look attractive. Not always physical death, but the stillness of giving up. There's a strange comfort in quitting. Dead things don't hurt anymore. A corpse doesn't feel rejection. A lifeless soul doesn't have to push through challenges or keep fighting battles. You can carry a sick person because they can still lean on you, still respond to help. But a corpse offers no cooperation at all. It is dead weight. That is how many live today: moving, but lifeless; existing, but empty; surviving but not thriving. They are carried by routine, carried by obligations, carried by the momentum of "just getting by," but there's no vitality, no passion, no spark of joy.

And right there, into that numb existence, Jesus interrupts with one word: *"Arise!"*

This word was not a suggestion. It was not an encouragement. It was a command spoken with the same authority that called light out of darkness and galaxies into being. Wherever Jesus spoke it, death itself lost its grip. When He declared "arise," heaven touched earth, and what was finished became unfinished, what was gone became restored, what was lost was given back.

Think about His ministry for a moment. Jesus did not spend much time at funerals, but the ones He attended, He ruined completely. Mourning was turned to dancing, lamentation to laughter, and death was forced to surrender its victims. Mourners left astonished, the devil left empty-handed, and the dead walked out alive.

> *And right there, into that numb existence, Jesus interrupts with one word: "Arise!"*

Take Jairus' daughter in Luke 8. She was young, full of potential, her life cut short before she could step into what God had destined for her. The house was filled with wailing and doubt. Jesus walked in, silenced the noise, and even put the mourners out of the room. Then He took the girl by the hand and said, *"Child, arise."* In an instant, breath returned. Her story was not over, because Jesus would not allow death to claim her before her time.

Or consider Lazarus in John 11. Four days in the tomb. The stench of death undeniable. Friends and family convinced it was too late. Yet Jesus commanded the stone rolled away, lifted His voice, and cried, *"Lazarus, come forth!"* Grave clothes fell away as a man bound by death shuffled back into the land of the living. What was written off as hopeless became the very stage for God's glory.

In Acts 9, even after Jesus had ascended, His resurrection power flowed through His disciples. Dorcas, also called Tabitha, was loved in her community, known for good works and kindness. Her sudden death devastated those around her. But when Peter arrived, he prayed and then spoke those same resurrection words: *"Tabitha, arise."* Her eyes opened, she sat up, and life returned so she could continue her assignment. Heaven declared what earth had tried to cut short: her time was not finished.

And then there is one of my favorite accounts, recorded in Luke 7, in the small town of Nain. A widow's only son was being carried to his burial. Her husband was already gone. Now her child was gone. In her culture, that meant her hope for the future was gone too. No provision. No protection. No legacy. She was left with a coffin instead of companionship, grief instead of joy, despair instead of a future. She walked behind the procession of death, surrounded by mourners who could not give her what she truly needed.

But at the city gate, everything shifted. The funeral crowd was leaving the town, heading toward the tomb. At the very same time, another crowd was entering, following Jesus, the Living One. Two processions met at the threshold: one led by death, one led by Life Himself. And Jesus did what He always does—He stepped into grief, touched what was untouchable, and spoke what no one expected: *"Young man, I say to you, arise!"* Immediately, the boy sat up and began to speak. The funeral turned into a reunion. The widow's despair turned into joy. And everyone present glorified God.

That story is a picture of what Jesus still does today. He meets us at the gate, at the thresholds of loss and despair, and speaks resurrection where everything feels final. He collides with the crowds of death that try to carry us away—grief, addiction, shame, brokenness—and He interrupts the procession with His authority.

And here is what modern readers need to hear: many of us are living at that same gate. Some are walking behind coffins of lost dreams, broken marriages, prodigal children, or crushed callings. Others are being carried by the crowd of despair, convinced that what they lost is gone forever. But Jesus still comes with His crowd—the crowd of life, hope, joy, and resurrection. And when the two collide, death must bow.

So, hear His word again: *"Arise!"* Do not let pressure suffocate your spirit. Do not let disappointment drown your hope. Do not let the enemy steal one more day of abundant life. Your story is not finished. Your time is not over. The procession toward the tomb is not your final destination. At the gate, Jesus meets you. And when He speaks, life comes rushing back.

OCCUPY YOUR PLACE AMONG THE LIVING

The Hebrew word for "time" in Ecclesiastes 7:17 is *eth*. That's not clock time, but an appointed season, an expected moment written by God Himself. It carries the weight of destiny, of divine scheduling, of a chapter already determined by the Author of life. When Scripture asks, *"Why should you die before your time?"* it isn't speaking about random accidents or vague possibility. It is pointing us toward the truth that God has marked a finish line for every life, and that line is wrapped in hope.

Jeremiah 29:11 makes it clear: *"For I know the plans I have for you, declares the Lord, plans for peace and not for evil, to give you a future and an expected end."* Notice those words, an *expected end*. Not chaos. Not despair. Not a premature cutoff. God declares the end from the beginning, which means He already knows how your story is supposed to conclude, and it is not in defeat. He alone reserves the right to determine when it is finished, not sin, not sickness, not tragedy, and not the schemes of the enemy.

Yet the reality is sobering: too many people die at 25 but aren't buried until 75. They stop living long before they stop breathing. Something breaks inside them, maybe a disappointment, a betrayal, a devastating failure, and they quietly shut down. Dreams fade. Joy evaporates. They go through motions, but life has already left their eyes. They bury their purpose while their body still moves. That is not the *eth* God has appointed. That is not the expected end He has written.

You matter more than you think. Your life is not a solitary flame, it is a torch that lights others. Someone you haven't even met yet may depend on your endurance. Someone's hope, someone's faith, someone's decision to keep going may be tied to the fact that you are still alive, still pressing forward, still refusing to quit.

> *You matter more than you think. Your life is not a solitary flame, it is a torch that lights others.*

That widow in Nain needed her son alive, not only for her comfort, but for her very survival. In her world, a woman without a husband or son was left destitute. His resurrection was not just about her broken heart; it was about her future security, her place in society, her ability to live. In the same way, your rising matters to more people than you realize. When you stop living, when you let despair silence your voice, the impact ripples far beyond you. But when you rise again, when you occupy your place among the living, hope multiplies.

When Jesus told the boy to *"arise,"* the Greek word He used was *egeiro*. It means more than simply "get up." It carries the sense of awakening, of being brought out of obscurity, of being caused to exist again. It means standing up and stepping back into the rightful place you were always meant to occupy. That's His word to you today: *Egeiro!* Awaken.

Get up. Step into your calling. Refuse to linger in shadows. Occupy your place among the living.

The boy's very first act after resurrection was to speak. Think about that. Maybe death had cut him off mid-sentence. Maybe there were words left unsaid, declarations unfinished, dreams half-voiced. But now, with breath restored, his voice returned. Resurrection gave him back his sound.

And that is exactly what God wants to do for you. Your voice matters. Your testimony matters. The enemy works hard to silence you through shame, through fear, and through pain, but when Jesus calls you to arise, He restores not only your life but your sound. It is time to speak again. It is time to declare life again. It is time to sing, to testify, to pray bold prayers, to speak words of hope that shift atmospheres.

Whatever has been diminishing you, whether sickness in your body, brokenness in your relationships, confusion in your work, or weariness in your spirit, God's power can reverse it. He is not intimidated by how long it has lasted. He is not limited by how final it looks. Romans 8:11 declares: *"The same Spirit who raised Jesus from the dead lives in you, and He will also give life to your mortal bodies."* The Spirit of resurrection is a living force inside you now, quickening what has grown weak, breathing vitality into what feels finished, reversing the momentum of death.

It is not your time to die. It is your time to live. Not to crawl through existence, but to rise with strength. Not to be carried by the crowd of despair, but to walk with the One who is Life Himself. Your *eth*, your appointed season, has not yet finished. Your expected end has not yet come, and until it does, you are called to stand, to speak, and to shine.

Hear His word over you today: *Egeiro!* Arise. Awaken. Occupy your place among the living.

7

Loss At The Gate

The gate is a strange place to meet God.

It's the in-between place, the boundary between what was and what will be. Between the safety of home and the uncertainties of the road. Between the city's life and the wilderness beyond. Gates are where people greet loved ones coming in, and where they say their last goodbyes to those going out.

In Luke 7:11–17, a mother walks toward that gate carrying the weight of her world in a coffin. Her only son is dead. Her husband is already gone. She has nothing left but the slow, terrible march toward burial. And at that very same gate, coming in from the opposite direction, walks Jesus.

Two crowds meet at a threshold, one following Life, the other following death.

THE CITY CALLED NAIN

Nain was not a place that most people in the first century would have considered remarkable. It was a small, hillside village in Galilee, tucked on the northern slope of the Hill of Moreh and overlooking the fertile sweep of the Jezreel Valley. The name itself meant *"pleasant"* or *"beautiful,"* suggesting a town that should have carried an atmosphere of peace and charm. But on the day recorded in Luke 7, beauty had given way to mourning. The streets were heavy with sorrow, the sound of wailing cut through the air, and the "pleasant place" became a setting of unbearable loss.

In Jesus' time, villages like Nain were close-knit in ways our modern world rarely experiences. Everyone knew one another. Families were interconnected, stories were shared openly, and sorrows were never carried in isolation. If tragedy struck a household, the entire town felt its weight. That is why the funeral we encounter in Luke 7 drew "a large crowd" from the city. They weren't spectators in the way we think of today. They were neighbors, friends, cousins, fellow laborers in the fields. The death of the widow's only son was not her grief alone; it was a wound that cut through the entire fabric of the community.

Luke tells us the procession made its way to the gate of the town. To us, that might sound like an incidental detail, but in the ancient world, gates carried deep meaning. Unlike the towering defensive gates of Jerusalem, Nain's gate was likely a simple arched entry point where the main road entered the settlement. But even a small gate was more than a door in a wall. It was a place of gathering, a kind of town square. The gate was where elders would sit to resolve disputes, travelers would be welcomed, and news would be exchanged. Gates were thresholds of life, weddings passed through them with joy, merchants passed through them with their goods, and armies sometimes passed through them with fear.

But on this day, the gate was marked by another kind of passage. A funeral procession moved out of the city, carrying sorrow with it. In the culture of the time, funerals were not quiet, private affairs. They were public events, with mourners lifting their voices in lament. Jewish burial happened quickly, often within the same day as the death itself. The body was washed carefully, anointed with spices to honor it, and wrapped in linen cloths. If the family had the means, professional mourners would be hired to add their wails and dirges, ensuring the grief was both heard and seen. To walk in that procession was to join in the collective acknowledgment that death had intruded again into the life of God's people.

The "coffin" mentioned in Luke's account was not what we think of in modern terms, a sealed wooden box. More likely, it was an open bier, a kind of stretcher or plank on which the wrapped body was carried. This open style of burial meant that those watching could see the form of the deceased as the procession passed. Family and friends surrounded it, their cries echoing off the stone walls of the houses, their hearts weighed down by the finality of what lay ahead. The road they walked was not random. It always led outside the town, for burial grounds were beyond the gate. Death had no place within the village itself. To carry someone past that threshold was to acknowledge an irreversible separation. Beyond the gate lay the tombs, the caves, the ground of the forgotten. Once you passed through, there was no turning back.

This is why Jesus' interruption is so profound. He meets them at the gate, in that narrow, liminal space between life and loss, between the last touch of a loved one and the silence of the grave. He doesn't wait until the burial is complete, until the stone is rolled across the tomb. He steps into the story while hope still flickers, however faintly. At the very place of transition, where the living and the dead, the city and the graveyard, hope and despair meet, Jesus arrives. He positions Himself at the threshold, reminding us that He always comes where the line seems most permanent.

And then comes the scandal. Luke tells us Jesus touched the bier. That act alone was startling, even offensive. According to the law in Numbers 19:11, anyone who touched a dead body, or even came into close contact with it, became ceremonially unclean for seven days. Religious leaders, rabbis, and scribes would have been careful to keep their distance. To touch the dead was to risk defilement, to risk exclusion from the rhythms of worship and temple life. It was something avoided, not embraced.

But Jesus does not recoil from death. He does not shrink back from impurity. Instead, He steps forward. His holiness is not fragile. It is not threatened by defilement. Where others feared contamination, Jesus carried a holiness that could not be corrupted. Death did not contaminate Him; He contaminated death. In that one touch, the entire order of things was reversed. Life flowed into what was lifeless. Purity overwhelmed impurity. Hope overpowered despair. Life flows outward. The flow of corruption is reversed. The One who is the Resurrection and the Life cannot be defiled by death; instead, death is undone by His touch.

In the Jewish imagination, death was the great enemy, the ultimate sign of human frailty and separation from God. Yet here stood Jesus, not only unafraid but authoritative. His touch did not dishonor Him, it revealed Him. It demonstrated that in Him was a power stronger than death itself. What the mourners thought was the end was, in His hands, only the beginning.

> *Death did not contaminate Him; He contaminated death.*

And so, the scene at Nain becomes more than a story about a widow and her son. It is a picture of the Gospel itself. The name of the village meant "pleasant" and "beautiful," but grief had stolen its meaning. Jesus restored it. At the threshold between loss and life, He rewrote the ending. That is who He is. He does not stand far off, waiting until we've buried our dreams, our hopes, or even ourselves. He meets us at the gate, at the place where life seems ready to give way to despair, and with one touch, one word, He interrupts the funeral march.

For every reader who has felt like the procession is moving forward without them, carrying away what they love most, this is good news. Jesus is not absent from your grief. He does not leave you to walk toward the grave alone. He comes to the very threshold, the very moment when it seems too late, and He places His hand where no one else dares. Because in Him, death is not the final authority.

TWO CROWDS AND A COLLISION

Luke paints the scene with vivid contrast:

"Now it happened, the day after, that He went into a city called Nain; and many of His disciples went with Him, and a large crowd. And when He came near the gate of the city, behold, a dead man was being carried out, the only son of his mother; and she was a widow. And a large crowd from the city was with her" (Luke 7:11–12).

Here are two processions moving in opposite directions. One is full of energy, curiosity, and expectation, disciples and townsfolk following Jesus, the miracle worker, the teacher, the healer. They laugh, they talk, they buzz with stories of what they've seen Him do. The other crowd walks in heavy silence, steps dragging to the rhythm of lament, carrying with them not only a body but also the broken heart of a widow whose last source of security has been ripped away. One procession is heading into the city with life; the other is headed out of it toward death.

The meeting point of these two crowds is the gate. It's no accident. It is a picture in motion, a living parable of how Jesus collides with human despair. At the very threshold where grief leads outward to the grave, life walks in to meet it. The gate becomes the arena where loss and hope, sorrow and salvation, death and life intersect.

Isn't that the story of our lives? We all have "gates." Gates are those places of transition, of decision, of painful collision between what we hoped for and what actually is. A hospital hallway, sterile and tense, as we wait for a doctor's report that could change everything. An HR office where the words "position eliminated" echo louder than any explanation. A courtroom door where the verdict about custody or sentencing will reshape an entire family's future. A phone call at midnight that takes our breath away before we even finish hearing the words. Gates are the thresholds of our lives, where faith and fear, life and loss, collide.

It is here, at the gate, that Jesus shows up. We often imagine that God meets us in holy places, in sanctuaries, in moments of worship or personal devotion. And He does. But Scripture also shows us that He meets us at gates, those messy, transitional, vulnerable places where we are least prepared for Him. Here, in Nain, Jesus writes resurrection into a widow's story not inside a temple, but at the dusty threshold of her greatest loss.

For the widow, this gate was the last step before finality. Once her son passed through, he would no longer belong to her home or her arms, but to the tomb. This was her last moment of nearness, her final goodbye. She had not asked Jesus to come. She had not cried out like blind Bartimaeus or fallen at His feet like Jairus. She was not seeking Him at all. She was drowning in her loss, carried forward by the momentum of grief.

But Jesus was there. That is the first miracle. She didn't go searching for Him; He came searching for her. She didn't pray a bold prayer of faith; she could barely walk. Yet He found her at her breaking point. And that is what He does still; He comes not only when we reach toward Him, but when we have no strength left to reach at all. He comes to those who cannot speak the words, who cannot hold themselves together, who cannot do anything but walk one step at a time toward the grave.

Psalm 34:18 says, *"The Lord is close to the brokenhearted and saves those who are crushed in spirit."* At Nain's gate, that verse comes alive. The Lord was not close to her because she had enough faith, or because she had prayed the right words, but simply because she was brokenhearted. His nearness is not earned, it is given.

> *She didn't go searching for Him; He came searching for her.*

Notice how the story unfolds: before He does anything for the son, Jesus does something for the mother. Verse 13 says, *"When the Lord saw her, He had compassion on her and said to her, 'Do not weep.'"* This order matters. Before He speaks resurrection to the dead, He speaks comfort to the living. Before He addresses the coffin, He acknowledges the one carrying the grief. He doesn't ignore her pain. He doesn't walk past her to get to the "main event." He stops, looks at her, and *sees* her.

This is not a passing glance. The Greek word for "saw" here means more than catching sight. It means to perceive deeply, to take in with full attention. He noticed her in her entirety...the lines on her face from years of widowhood, the emptiness in her eyes from losing her last anchor, the trembling in her body from exhaustion. He saw the entire weight of her loss.

Then comes compassion. The word used here is one of the strongest in the New Testament. It literally means to be moved in the deepest parts of your being, to feel something so powerfully that it stirs you into action. Whenever this word appears in the Gospels, it almost always describes Jesus. His compassion is not polite sympathy or distant pity. It is visceral, gut-wrenching love that compels Him to step into our suffering.

Here is the pattern of heaven: compassion before power. Before He raises the son, He comforts the mother. Before He performs the miracle, He shares the pain. Compassion is the miracle's foundation. Jesus does not heal out of cold authority; He heals out of burning love.

And in that moment, at that gate, two crowds collided, but only one continued forward. The crowd of death stopped in its tracks, interrupted by the crowd of life. Grief met grace. Finality met resurrection. And the widow who thought she was walking toward an ending discovered that she was standing at a new beginning.

"DO NOT WEEP"

At first, the words almost sound offensive. *"Do not weep."* How could anyone say that to a mother whose only son has just died? How could those words possibly bring comfort in the middle of such devastation? If anyone else had said them, they might have sounded shallow, dismissive, or even cruel. But when Jesus speaks, His words are never empty. He does not say *"do not weep"* because He wants her to suppress her emotions or pretend that her pain isn't real. He says it because He is about to remove the cause of her tears. His command is a promise.

That is the difference between human consolation and divine intervention. People say, *"don't cry,"* because they are uncomfortable with sorrow or feel powerless to help. Jesus says, *"do not weep,"* because He carries within Himself the authority to rewrite the story. He does not minimize her mourning; He interrupts it. And that distinction matters. The widow at Nain had every reason to weep. She had already buried her husband and now faced burying her only son. Her tears were the most rational response to crushing loss. But Jesus does not simply wipe away tears; He transforms the reason for them.

Then the narrative takes a shocking turn. Verse 14 says: *"Then He came and touched the open coffin, and those who carried him stood still."* That touch stops everything. The bearers halt mid-step. The mourners grow silent. The two crowds, one full of hope, one full of despair, suddenly freeze in breathless anticipation. Time itself seems to stand still.

> *Jesus says, "do not weep," because He carries within Himself the authority to rewrite the story.*

What happens next is staggering in its simplicity. No elaborate ritual. No priestly chants. No appeal to heaven. No outward display of effort. Just the sheer authority of a spoken word: *"Young man, I say to you, arise!"* He speaks directly to the dead boy as if he can hear Him—because he can. The voice that called light into being at creation now calls life back into a lifeless body. The same Word through whom all things were made now commands what was broken to be restored. And death obeys.

The response is immediate: *"So he who was dead sat up and began to speak."* Imagine the gasp in the crowd as the motionless figure stirred, sat upright, and then opened his mouth. Speaking was more than a sign of movement; it was evidence of soul, of identity, of restored humanity. For this widow, her last conversation with her son had ended in silence. Now she hears his voice again. It is the restoration of relationship, the renewal of life not just in his body but in their bond.

Jesus then does something profoundly tender: *"And He presented him to his mother."* That moment is everything. He does not keep the son as evidence of His power. He does not parade him as proof of His divinity. He gives him back. The miracle is relational. The glory of God takes shape not in spectacle alone but in restoration...restoration of family, restoration of hope, and restoration of future.

What is the reaction of the people? Luke says, *"Then fear came upon all, and they glorified God, saying, 'A great prophet has risen up among us'; and 'God has visited His people.'"* The word *fear* here is not about terror but awe. It is the deep reverence that comes when you suddenly realize you are standing in the presence of Someone who holds authority over life and death itself. The people recognize that they are encountering the visitation of God. The ordinary has been invaded by the extraordinary. The finality of the grave has been interrupted by the eternity of heaven.

Praise erupts. Grief turns to glory. The wailing that once filled the air is replaced by worship. They cannot help but glorify God because when life walks into death's path, the only reasonable response is awe and gratitude. Notice that the crowd does not merely celebrate the son's return, they glorify the God who made it happen. True encounters with Jesus always turn attention away from the gift itself and back toward the Giver.

The widow had come to the gate expecting only to lose. She left it carrying her son's hand again, her tears turned from sorrow to joy. The crowd had gathered to bury, but instead they found themselves praising. That is the power of Jesus' words: *"Do not weep."* He never says it lightly. He never says it cheaply. He says it because He alone has the power to turn mourning into dancing, ashes into beauty, despair into praise.

MEETING US AT OUR GATES TODAY

This story is not locked in the dusty streets of first-century Nain. It is a pattern, a living testimony of how Jesus still moves at the gates of our lives today. Gates are those thresholds where life and loss collide, where one step feels like hope and the next like finality. They are the places where we stand trembling between what we once believed possible and what we now fear is over.

For some, the gate looks like a divorce hearing. You walk into that courtroom knowing that what you once vowed before God and man is now being carried out like a corpse, and it feels as though your family is being buried with the papers. For others, the gate is the foreclosure notice taped to the door, the end of stability, the shattering of a dream you built brick by brick, now slipping away. For someone else, the gate is not in a courtroom or at a house, but in the quiet anguish of watching a friend or child walk away from faith, leaving you holding unanswered prayers like a funeral dirge in your chest. We all have gates. They look different, but they feel the same: heavy, final, and irreversible.

And yet, the lesson from Nain breaks through the centuries to reach us. Jesus is not absent from your pain. The widow didn't send for Him. She didn't pray a long prayer or make a desperate appeal. She was too lost in her grief to even look up. But Jesus sought her out. He walked into her sorrow, uninvited yet utterly intentional. That is who He is, the Shepherd who leaves the ninety-nine to find the one. When you can't find the strength to reach for Him, He still reaches for you.

He also meets us at the threshold. He doesn't always wait until we have tidied our grief or composed our souls. He steps right into the space where mourning is loud, where disappointment still stings, where the coffin is still being carried. He doesn't sidestep the mess; He walks straight into it. This is the Jesus who enters hospital rooms, courtroom verdicts, bank foreclosures, and sleepless nights. He does not shy away from the gates of our despair. He turns them into altars of encounter.

> *He does not shy away from the gates of our despair. He turns them into altars of encounter.*

And when He arrives, He brings compassion and power together. Many of us believe in one or the other. We think God feels for us but does not intervene, or that He has power but is cold and distant. The story of Nain shows both; He sees deeply, and He acts decisively. He doesn't scold the grieving or lecture the broken. He looks, He feels, He is moved, and then He commands. His tears and His authority are never at odds. Compassion fuels power. Love becomes action.

That's why He can speak resurrection into hopelessness. When He opened His mouth that day and said, *"Young man, I say to you, arise!"* the funeral ended. Mourning turned to marvel. The lifeless sat up and spoke. That voice still echoes today. The same Jesus speaks into dead marriages, into lifeless callings, into suffocated dreams, into hearts that have gone numb from disappointment. His word carries weight that no grave can resist.

This is where it comes home, your turn at the gate. Some of us are walking in the funeral procession right now. We are carrying the coffin of dreams we've declared gone, relationships we've pronounced beyond repair, callings we've left buried because disappointment convinced us they were over. We're convinced the only destination is the tomb. Yet, on the other side of the road, Jesus is walking toward us. And when He meets us, He will do what He always does: He will look at us, really see us. Not the polished version we show others, not the mask we wear in church, but the real us, eyes swollen from tears, shoulders slumped under grief. He sees.

Then He will touch the coffin. The thing you thought was untouchable. The place you've guarded, the wound you've been afraid to let anyone near. He will put His hand there, not to shame you, not to wound you further, but to stop the march toward the grave. And then He will speak. His voice will break through despair with the command of heaven: *"Arise."*

And when He speaks, dead things sit up. They live. They move. They speak again. What you thought would never recover begins to breathe. What you thought was gone forever is handed back into your arms, not as a memory but as a miracle. That is what He does at the gate.

But here is the crucial question; will you let Him interrupt? Will you allow Him to stop the funeral march of your heart? Will you let Him touch the places of loss you've kept hidden? Will you risk hope again when you've already made peace with despair? The widow didn't ask for the interruption, but when it came, it changed everything. It can change everything for you too, if you will let Him.

8

Sticking With Jesus

The greatest miracle of all is salvation and eternity with God. Every healing, every provision, every breakthrough points toward this one, eternal reality. Some will press through the crowd for a temporary blessing but walk away when they discover what "all in" truly costs. Yet there is no greater miracle than the moment a soul turns fully toward Christ and remains with Him through storms, through offense, and through testing. The Bible calls salvation impossible for man, but possible for God. It is the miracle that outlasts every other miracle, and the only one that will still matter ten thousand years from now.

That is why this chapter begins with a question: *Will you press in for the greatest miracle, or will you be satisfied with something less?*

The crowds that followed Jesus often began with excitement, drawn by what they had seen or heard. They came because sick bodies were healed and empty stomachs were filled. They came because water turned into wine and the lame walked. But when the teaching turned sharp, when the cost of discipleship rose, when Jesus spoke of total surrender, the crowds thinned fast.

It happened in John 6, right after one of the most famous miracles in the Gospels, the feeding of over five thousand people with a boy's small lunch. The people were so amazed that they started comparing Jesus to Moses, the prophet who had brought bread from heaven and led Israel into the promised land. Some wanted to make Him king. But Jesus knew they misunderstood His mission, so He withdrew to pray alone on a mountain before joining His disciples on the lake.

The next day the crowd caught up with Him in Capernaum. Jesus did not greet them with flattery. Instead, He asked, *"Why are you following Me? Is it because you truly believe, or because you want more bread?"* They answered with their request: *Do the miracle again. Give us bread from heaven.*

His reply was both an invitation and a dividing line: *"I am the bread of life. Whoever comes to Me will never hunger, and whoever believes in Me will never thirst."*

The crowd's minds were still on their own ideas of who Jesus was supposed to be and what He was supposed to do. But Jesus pressed further, teaching about abiding in Him, about receiving Him fully, the way bread becomes part of you when you eat it. He spoke in words that stripped away casual interest: *"Unless you eat the flesh of the Son of Man and drink His blood, you have no life in you."*

He was not talking about communion. Remember that the cross had not yet happened. He was not calling for cannibalism or strange ritual. He was calling for absolute faith, loyalty, and commitment. This was a message about believing so completely that His life becomes your life, His heart your heart, His ways your ways. It was about grafting yourself into Him like a branch into a vine, so that no part of you can exist apart from Him.

But as soon as the words left His mouth, the mood shifted. What had been awe became offence. John tells us that many of His disciples said, *"This is a hard saying; who can accept it?"* The Greek word for "hard" here carries the sense of "scandalous" or "too much to ask." They did not misunderstand Him, they understood perfectly well that He was demanding their whole life.

Jesus knew they were grumbling. And He did not soften His teaching to make them stay. Instead, He asked, *"Does this offend you? What will you do when you see the Son of Man ascend to where He was before? It is the Spirit who gives life; the flesh profits nothing. The words I speak are spirit and life."*

And then came the moment that would empty the stadium. John records, *"From that time many of His disciples turned back and no longer followed Him."* In the space of one sermon, Jesus went from a crowd of thousands to a small circle of twelve.

He turned to them and asked the question that still echoes today: *"Do you also want to go away?"*

Simon Peter's reply rings like a battle cry for every believer who has faced the temptation to turn back: *"Lord, to whom shall we go? You have the words of eternal life. We have come to believe and know that You are the Holy One of God."*

Peter did not have all the answers. He did not know the full weight of the cross that lay ahead. But he knew enough to cling to Jesus when the crowd was walking away. That is the heart of sticking with Jesus.

Peter's bold declaration was a decision to stay when others left. That is the fork in the road every believer eventually comes to. When the cost becomes clear, when the crowd starts moving in the opposite direction, when following Christ is no longer convenient, will you still be there?

Following Jesus has never been about blending into the majority. The crowd is fickle. The same multitude that shouted "Hosanna" on Sunday shouted, "Crucify Him!" by Friday. Popular opinion can turn on a dime, and salvation has never been decided by public vote. Commitment to Christ is not the consensus of a group—it is the conviction of a heart.

In John 6, the issue was never bread. It was always about belief. Jesus was not looking for people who enjoyed the show; He was looking for those who would abide in Him when there was no bread, no fish, no spectacle—only surrender. He was calling them to stop circling the signs and start moving toward the destination those signs pointed to.

Crowds can be impressed by miracles without ever seeking the Miracle-Worker. They can cheer at blessings but choke on commitment. And if you're not careful, the crowd's comfort can pull you away from Christ's call.

Even today, many approach faith like those Galilean crowds, excited about the benefits, but hesitant about the demands. We want the healing but not the holiness. We want the provision but not the pruning. We want the power but not the price. But the kingdom is not built on half-measures. He is Lord or He is nothing.

> *Crowds can be impressed by miracles without ever seeking the Miracle-Worker.*

That is why sometimes you have to step *out* of the crowd to stay *with* Christ.

OUT OF THE CROWD

John 6 begins with anticipation in the air. A massive crowd had gathered, thousands of people converging on a hillside because they had seen Jesus heal the sick. Word had spread quickly that this man could do what no one else could. Families carried the ill on mats, neighbors whispered about miracles, children clung to their parents, wide-eyed with hope. The atmosphere was electric with longing. Maybe today He would heal their child. Maybe today He would restore their body. Maybe today He would lift the crushing burden they carried.

Jesus did not disappoint them. With nothing more than a boy's small lunch, five loaves and two fish, He multiplied the food until every single person ate their fill, with twelve baskets of leftovers gathered afterward. It was a miracle so stunning that the people tried to make Him king by force. They wanted a leader who could keep multiplying bread, who could keep filling their bellies and fixing their problems.

But here's the tension: they loved the miracle, but they missed the meaning. They wanted the bread, not the Bread of Life. They saw provision, but not the Person standing before them. They were caught up in what He could do, but blind to who He truly was. They clung to the gift without seeing the Giver. To them, this was a service to be repeated, not a sign pointing to a greater reality. That same danger is alive today. We can chase God for what He gives and forget who He is. We can clutch at blessings as though they're the goal, forgetting that every answered prayer, every provision, every healing is meant to draw us closer to Him. A road sign is a pointer. No one builds a house under a sign that says "Jerusalem, 10 miles." Yet many settle under the signs of miracles rather than walking the road to the Miracle Worker.

The crowd wanted His hand, but not His heart. They wanted bread without brokenness, blessing without surrender, a kingdom without a cross. And when Jesus shifted from multiplying loaves to saying, *"I am the bread of life. Unless you eat My flesh and drink My blood, you have no life in you"* (John 6:35, 53), everything changed. The mood shifted. Murmurs rose. Offense spread. They wanted Him to fill their baskets, not redefine their very existence. This is where the line is always drawn. Fans enjoy the benefits, but disciples embrace the cost.

The miracle of the loaves and fish didn't begin with plenty. It didn't start with overflowing storerooms or a wealthy donor's generosity. It began with one boy who offered his lunch. He didn't wait until he had more. He didn't analyze whether it was enough.

He simply placed it in Jesus' hands and Jesus multiplied it. That's how faith works throughout Scripture. Peter had to step out of the boat before he walked on water. The blind man had to wash in the pool before his eyes opened. Faith is not passive! It moves, it risks, and it participates.

Fans enjoy the benefits, but disciples embrace the cost.

But the crowd that day wasn't interested in participation. They were content to spectate. They wanted to enjoy the miracle without offering anything of their own. They wanted to stay close enough to witness the action but far enough to avoid the cost. That's the subtle danger of being in the crowd—you can be near Jesus without ever being changed by Him. And that danger lingers in modern life. It's possible to sit in church every week, sing the songs, hear the Word, and yet never step out of the crowd. It's possible to admire the miracles in someone else's life while never offering your own "five loaves and two fish." Crowds don't require commitment. Fans don't have to sacrifice. But Jesus is not looking for spectators. He is looking for disciples who will bring what they have, however small, and trust Him to make it more.

The shift in John 6 is dramatic. One day, Jesus is feeding thousands, and the people are buzzing with excitement. The next, He is teaching about sacrifice and surrender, and the enthusiasm drains from the air. Laughter dies down. Whispers spread. People frown at one another in disbelief: *Did He really say that? Does He mean it literally? Can we follow a man who speaks this way?* It wasn't that they misunderstood Him, it was that they understood, and they couldn't accept it. They wanted a Messiah who fit their expectations, who would bless them on their terms. But Jesus offered Himself, and for many, that was too much.

So, they left. Some drifted away quietly. Others turned with open offense. Some lingered on the edges, torn between desire and doubt. But by the end, the crowd was gone. And then Jesus turned to the twelve. With piercing honesty, He asked: *"Do you also want to go away?"*

That question still hangs in the air today. When following Jesus stops being popular, when it costs your reputation, your comfort, your standing, will you stay? When obedience requires forgiving the unforgivable, loving the unlovable, giving when it hurts, will you still be there? The easy faith of the crowd fades when the cost becomes clear. The call to discipleship is not about full baskets but about full surrender. It is about moving from the excitement of miracles to the endurance of obedience.

Peter's answer must become ours: *"Lord, to whom shall we go? You have the words of eternal life."* Crowds may thin. Miracles may draw some but offend others. But those who stay discover the deepest truth: the real miracle is not in the bread, but in the Bread of Life Himself.

CRAZY ENOUGH TO STAY

Faith that clings to Jesus no matter the cost will always look extreme to the world. There is even a phrase the early church used to describe it—divine madness. Outsiders see it and shake their heads. To them it seems irrational to give your whole life to someone you cannot see, to obey commands that push against culture, to resist the current of the majority when the majority appears safe and comfortable. Why keep going when others have walked away? Why stay when staying costs more than leaving?

The reason is simple, though not always easy: because faith has tuned its ear to a different frequency. The world hears only noise, but the believer hears the Shepherd's voice. Others wonder why you keep dancing when no music is playing, but you know you are moving to a song that heaven itself is singing. The crowd is driven by trends, fear, and convenience, but discipleship requires a different compass. Faith does not take its cues from the mass opinion of the crowd; it listens to the One who calls your name.

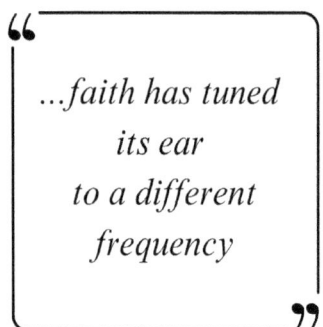

...faith has tuned its ear to a different frequency

And here is the paradox: sticking with Jesus will not always lead you along the broad and bustling road. More often, it will draw you into paths that are narrower, harder, and lonelier. His way rarely looks like a shortcut. It often feels like the long way around. But those who stay discover something that cannot be found anywhere else - that this narrow road, though it costs more, leads to life that cannot be shaken.

Peter's story on the water captures this truth in vivid detail. The storm was fierce, the waves relentless, the wind howling across the night. The boat offered some sense of security, even if it was tossing and groaning under the weight of the storm. Logic said, Stay put. Wait until morning. But Peter saw Jesus walking across the sea, and suddenly the boat didn't feel as safe anymore. The safest place was not where it was stable—it was wherever Jesus was, even if that meant stepping onto the waves.

Peter's step out of the boat was reckless by human standards, but it was obedience by heaven's measure. And Jesus did not scold him for leaving the boat. He didn't say, "You should have stayed where it was secure." Instead, when Peter faltered, Jesus' words were, *"Why did you doubt?"* In other words: *You were doing it. You were walking on water. You were stepping into the miraculous. Don't stop now.*

That's what faith does, it grows when we step beyond comfort zones into places where only God can hold us. Worship on the boat is good, but the deepest trust is forged in the howling wind and the rolling sea. Following Jesus is already a call to walk on water. Every act of obedience that costs you something, every decision to hold His Word when everything else shakes, every moment you refuse to give up, you are doing what Peter did. You are walking on waves.

But the waves are not the hardest part. The hardest part is realizing that most people will never leave the boat. The majority will stay with the crowd. They will follow when it's easy and turn back when it's hard. Jesus spoke plainly about this in Matthew 7: the wide road is always more popular, but it ends in destruction. The narrow way feels lonely at times, but it is the only road that leads to life. John 6 shows this in stark detail. Thousands ate the bread. Dozens chased the signs. But when Jesus called for surrender, when He said, *"Eat my flesh and drink my blood,"* they could not accept it. One by one, the crowd dissolved until only a handful remained.

And here's what is striking: Jesus didn't chase after them. He didn't soften His teaching to make it easier. He didn't say, "Wait, let me offer a simpler version of discipleship." He let them walk away. Then He turned to the twelve with that piercing question: *"Do you also want to go away?"*

We measure success by numbers, but Jesus measures it by obedience. We call it revival when a room is packed; He calls it revival when hearts are surrendered. Numbers swell easily, obedience rarely does. Before almost every major move of God in Scripture, there was a refining. Gideon's army shrank from thousands to three hundred before the victory. The disciples hid in an upper room before Pentecost turned the world upside down. The early church scattered under persecution before it multiplied across nations. Purity almost always precedes power.

That means you should not be afraid if the crowd around you thins. Don't fear if others walk away when the cost of discipleship becomes too high. You may look foolish to the world for staying when it would be easier to go, but sometimes being "crazy enough to stay" is the truest sanity. Because when the storm clears and the waves calm, the only ones still standing will be those who never stopped walking toward Jesus.

Purity almost always precedes power.

LUKEWARM FAITH

The greatest danger to the church has never been open rebellion alone, it has always been lukewarm faith. Jesus' words in Revelation 3 are startling: *"Because you are lukewarm, neither hot nor cold, I am about to spit you out of My mouth."* The warning was spoken to Laodicea, a wealthy city whose very name means *"the people's opinion."* How fitting. The danger was not that the church there had collapsed into blatant paganism, but that their faith had grown tame, shaped more by convenience and comfort than by conviction. They had learned how to blend in, to manage appearances, to keep enough religion to look spiritual but not enough fire to be surrendered.

That's what makes lukewarmness so insidious, it hides under a veneer of faith. It's not the outright denial of Christ but the slow replacement of devotion with distraction. The Laodiceans had riches, but no zeal. They had influence, but no intimacy. They were well regarded by people but nauseating to the Lord. And it is sobering to realize that Jesus found half-hearted faith more offensive than outright rejection. Cold could still be awakened, but lukewarm was satisfied with its own temperature.

We see this danger in John 6 as well. After the bread was multiplied, the crowd celebrated the miracle but stumbled over the message. When Jesus declared, *"Unless you eat My flesh and drink My blood, you have no life in you,"* it cut against their expectations. This wasn't about a ritual meal, it was about total union with Him. To take Him in fully. To abide so completely that His life became their life. That was too much for many. So, they left. They didn't necessarily storm away in outrage; they simply drifted back to what was familiar, to what required no surrender. And that's the terrifying part. They didn't run to idols; they returned to normal life. But sometimes "normal" is the most dangerous place to be, because it lulls us into thinking we can have Christ on our terms.

That is lukewarm faith today. It is easy to wear the label of Christian while living as though the cross makes no demands. It is possible to attend services, know the songs, even speak the language of faith while keeping the jar of oil sealed tight. Lukewarm faith is more about convenience than commitment, more about what fits in than what follows Christ. It is polite but powerless, comfortable but compromised.

Jesus never called people to visit Him when convenient. He called them to abide. To abide is more than checking in with Him in moments of crisis; it is to graft your life into His as a branch to a vine. It is to let His Word infiltrate your thoughts, His Spirit shape your desires, His ways transform your actions until your life cannot be untangled from His. This is why His words in John 6 sounded so radical: He was not offering spiritual snacks; He was inviting complete assimilation. The crowd tripped over it, but the disciples stayed because they knew, even without understanding, that life was found nowhere else.

> *It is polite but powerless, comfortable but compromised.*

And that is where every believer eventually comes to a defining moment. Jesus may not ask you aloud, *"Do you also want to go away?"* but life will. The question comes in disguised forms—when your prayer goes unanswered, when obedience costs more than you planned, when following Him sets you against public opinion or even your own family's approval. That's when lukewarm faith falls away, and only surrendered faith remains.

Peter's answer is the one that echoes through the ages: *"Lord, to whom shall we go? You have the words of eternal life."* Notice he did not say, "We understand everything You're saying." He didn't. The cross was still ahead, the resurrection unimagined, the Spirit not yet poured out. But he knew enough. He knew that whatever mysteries remained, life was only found in Christ. And so, he stayed.

This is what real discipleship looks like. Not having all the answers but having the right allegiance. Not fully grasping every mystery but refusing to let go of the One who holds them. To stay when others leave is not simply an act of loyalty, it is an act of worship. It is saying with your life, *"I would rather be bewildered with Jesus than comfortable without*

Him. I would rather wrestle with unanswered questions in His presence than live in the crowd's easy explanations apart from Him."

And here is the truth that cuts across every age: the miracle beyond the crowd is not the bread, not the fish, not even the spectacular healings. The greatest miracle is the soul that abides in Christ to the very end. Many receive provision. Many see wonders. But only those who endure find the miracle of salvation...the new birth, the unshakable hope, the eternal life that does not end when the crowd disperses.

So let the crowd drift if it must. Let convenience call them back to their comforts. Stay. Stay when worship costs you your pride. Stay when faith costs you your reputation. Stay when obedience costs you everything you thought you wanted. Because the One you are staying with is worth more than all that could be lost. On the other side of that costly devotion, you will discover what the lukewarm never will, that Jesus Himself is the reward.

Conclusion

A HEART MADE NEW

The Gospels are filled with miracles. We have walked through them together; blind eyes opened, lepers cleansed, paralytics walking, storms calmed, demons driven out, and the dead raised. We have stood in the crowd and watched Jesus lay His hand on the untouchable. We have seen Him stop funerals in their tracks and turn mourning into dancing. We have watched Him speak a word and turn a life around in an instant. Each scene has pulled us into the wonder of a God who steps into human brokenness with authority and compassion.

Every healing has been a moment of heaven breaking into earth, of the eternal touching the temporary. But beneath the applause of the crowd and the astonishment of the disciples, there is something deeper, an invitation that outlasts the moment. Every miracle points beyond itself, like a road sign directing us somewhere greater. The miracles matter, but they are not the final destination. The ultimate miracle is not when a body is restored for a lifetime, but when a heart is made new for eternity.

Think of it: the man lowered through the roof in Mark 2 received more than the strength to walk. Before his legs were healed, Jesus looked at him and said, *"Your sins are forgiven."* That is the miracle that outlasts bones and muscles. In John 11, Lazarus came back from the grave, it was a glimpse of resurrection life, a preview of the day when death itself would be defeated. The woman at the well in John 4 thought she was coming for water. Instead, she walked away with living water that could never run dry. Over and over again, Jesus revealed that He came to make all things new.

This is the miracle that Nicodemus struggled to understand in John 3. Jesus told him, "*You must be born again.*" Not try harder. Not be a little better. Not polish up your reputation. Something far more radical: you must receive a brand-new life. Paul would later describe it this way: "*If anyone is in Christ, he is a new creation; the old has gone, the new has come.*" A healed body may run for a season, but a new heart will run into eternity. A calm mind may last for a lifetime, but a redeemed soul will live forever.

This is what makes salvation the greatest miracle. It is not about improving the old you, it is about raising the dead you. Ezekiel prophesied that God would take away hearts of stone and replace them with hearts of flesh, alive to Him. That is what Jesus does. He doesn't patch over our brokenness; He gives us His own Spirit, His own life. The leper went home with clear skin, but the disciple went out with a new purpose. The demoniac sat clothed and in his right mind, but more than that, he became a messenger of good news. The miracle of salvation is not only what Jesus removes from us, that is shame, guilt, and fear, but what He fills us with: joy, peace, and His very presence.

If you look closely, you'll see that not everyone who experienced a miracle in the Gospels became a follower of Jesus. Ten lepers were healed; only one returned to give thanks. Thousands ate bread in the wilderness, but when the teaching became hard, most walked away. Miracles

> *It is not about improving the old you, it is about raising the dead you.*

may draw a crowd but only surrender makes a disciple. The ones who stayed close to Him were the ones transformed from the inside out. Peter, once afraid of a servant girl's question, became a bold witness to thousands. Mary Magdalene, once tormented, became the first to declare that the tomb was empty. Matthew, once chained to greed, became an evangelist writing the story of the King.

That is the choice that still stands before each of us. Will you settle for admiring Jesus from the crowd, or will you step out to follow Him? The crowd is curious, even inspired, but also fickle. Crowds cheer on Sunday and crucify on Friday. Crowds want bread but balk at surrender. Jesus is not calling for spectators; He is calling for followers. To step out of the crowd is to echo Peter's words: "Lord, to whom shall we go? You have the words of eternal life."

The invitation is for you, right now. The same Jesus who reached for the widow at Nain reaches for you. The same One who raised Jairus's daughter can raise your spirit from despair. The same compassion that touched outcasts still stretches toward every weary heart. Salvation is about being joined to Christ. It is not about becoming a slightly improved version of yourself; it is about receiving His life in exchange for your own.

The Bible makes it plain: "If you confess with your mouth that Jesus is Lord and believe in your heart that God raised Him from the dead, you will be saved." To confess Him as Lord is to hand Him the steering wheel of your life. To believe is to trust Him completely—not only with your eternity but with your today. Maybe you've been in the crowd a long time, admiring Him from a distance, or maybe you once walked with Him but drifted back. Either way, He is calling you now.

What do you need to do?

First, acknowledge your need. Every one of us has sinned and fallen short of God's glory. We cannot fix ourselves.

Second, believe in Jesus. He is the way, the truth, and the life. Believe that His death was for you, His resurrection is for you, His life is for you.

Third, surrender. Give Him your plans, your pride, your failures, your future. Say, "I am Yours." And fourth, follow Him daily, a lifelong journey of walking in His steps.

If your heart is ready, you can express that surrender in prayer. You might say something like this:

Lord Jesus, I believe You are the Son of God. I believe You died for my sins and rose again to give me life. I confess that I am a sinner in need of Your grace. Today I turn from my old life and place my trust in You. Come into my heart, make me new, and be the Lord of my life. I will follow You from this day forward. Thank You for the gift of salvation. Amen.

If you prayed that sincerely, then according to God's promise, you have received the greatest miracle of all. Heaven itself rejoices when even one sinner repents. Think about that...your decision has set off celebration in the presence of angels. Your name is written in the Book of Life. You are no longer dead in sin; you are alive in Christ. You are no longer lost; you are found.

This miracle won't make earthly headlines, but it is the greatest headline in heaven. And it is only the beginning! The One who began this good work in you will carry it through to completion. You are stepping into transformation, a lifelong journey of becoming more like Him. Along the way, your story will ripple into the lives of others. Someone else may find hope because of the hope that now fills you. Someone else may encounter Christ because you chose to walk with Him.

The final miracle is not the healing of a body, the calming of a storm, or even the raising of the dead. The final miracle is that Jesus takes a heart of stone and gives a heart of flesh. He takes the sinner's name and writes it in His book forever. He makes you new, and what He makes new will never wear out, never fade, and never be taken away.

The crowd may move on. The world may turn its back. But you, once dead and now alive, will walk with the One who is the same yesterday, today, and forever, and that is the greatest miracle of all.

Other Books by Nico Smit

Nico Smit has also written It's Time To Go Up!, Revival People and Gilgal To Bethel; available wherever books are sold online

Also available by Nico Smit:
Nico Smit's blog: nicosmitblog.com

www.ingramcontent.com/pod-product-compliance
Lightning Source LLC
Chambersburg PA
CBHW061209070526
44583CB00025B/3180